PRESSURE IS
A PRIVILEGE

Praise for *Pressure Is a Privilege*

I've known Billie Jean King since she was twelve years old. I've seen a wise fighter in her every year since. Billie was No. 1 in the world on the tennis court, No. 1 in fighting for women's causes, and the No. 1 advocate for women's rights in sports. If I had a nickel for everything Billie Jean has done to help the sport of tennis-all for free-I would be a rich man. *Pressure Is a Privilege* will help everyone through some tough times.

–Vic Braden, Tennis Coach and Author

Pressure Is a Privilege is exhilarating, and a good tonic for the human spirit! It is full of lifelong battles and lessons-it's about belief, it's about commitment, it's about putting yourself on the line. I would often hear "Pressure is a privilege!" during match point when Billie and I shared the court in doubles. Many of us see pressure as a burden, not a privilege, but Billie Jean lived for these moments and would rise to the occasion like no one I've ever seen. She is a warrior on and off the court; there are no greater victories than those fought under pressure and against all odds, and this she's done very well. I congratulate her on converting me to the idea that pressure is a privilege.

–Rosie Casals, King's Doubles Partner,
  Member of the Original Nine

No one in sport ever faced more pressure than Billie Jean King. No one ever learned how to deal with it better than her. And now, no one has ever described how to deal with it better than her. It's a privilege for us all to have the chance to learn from Billie Jean.

–Frank Deford, Author and Commentator

You don't become No. 1 in the world at anything unless you live it. Now, Billie Jean King has really written the book on it and, in doing so, teaches us how we can be No. 1 in whatever we want to do.

–Chris Evert, Hall of Fame Tennis Legend

One of America's best athletes of all time has written a wonderful book. Few people in my lifetime have seen the world change as she has, but she has never lost faith in truth and justice. *Pressure Is a Privilege* is a must-read for anyone who decides to reach for the stars. Family, friends, and country have been her strength; she is a real hero and has not been ashamed to tell all. Buy this book, and take a journey with my good friend, Billie Jean King.

–George Foreman, World Heavyweight Champ,
King's Impromptu Body Guard at the Battle of the Sexes

Let this book and all of its teachings be a source of strength for all of us who face various pressures in our daily life. This is clearly Billie Jean's mission as she continues to build on her legend as an inspiration and a guidance counselor for people all over the world.

–Ross Greenburg, President, HBO Sports

It's easy to look at someone like Billie Jean King and believe she is impervious to the human frailties that hound us mere mortals. In fact, her name alone has become some sort of cultural shorthand for mental toughness and steely resolve. But when you read this book you realize Billie Jean was once just another little girl from Long Beach who was just as afraid, just as vulnerable, and just as uncertain as the rest of us. And you realize, too, that this is where her true greatness lies. Because Billie Jean's story is not so much the story of a towering, historic figure who forever changed the world; it's the story of a young woman who, on a hot Texas night in 1973, with so much hanging in the balance, somehow found the strength and the courage to do it.

–Sheila C. Johnson, President and Managing
Partner of the Washington Mystics, co-founder of BET

Billie Jean King is an inspiration! In this book she shares her life experiences to help you discover the happiness and success that is right in front of you. Bobby Riggs also comes out a winner in the Battle of the Sexes because of Billie Jean King's tips on handling the daily challenges and pressures of life.

—Lornie Kuhle, Bobby Riggs's Coach at the Battle of the Sexes

Billie Jean's unbridled energy, enthusiasm, and intensity to anything she puts her mind to amazes me to this day. No wonder that has translated to success. If we all cared that much, the world would be in better shape.

—John McEnroe, Tennis Legend, Television Commentator

Billie Jean King is a true American hero, one who has inspired untold numbers of girls to go for their goals. In this book, she lets us in on some of the secrets of her own success, combining great stories with genuinely good advice. By putting it all on paper, King expands her role as a mentor for individual young women to the wider world of readers who can absorb a great deal of wisdom from these pages.

—Cokie Roberts, Political Analyst for ABC News
and NPR, Author of *Ladies of Liberty*

Billie Jean King made it possible for generations of women to be strong, powerful, and have a voice. She believed in me when I was fourteen and she always supports me today. This book is like having a personal conversation with Billie Jean, as she teaches us how to navigate the pressures of the tough times and manage the opportunities and challenges of the good times. She is a friend, an icon, and a living example of the good things that come to you when you put others before yourself.

—Maria Sharapova, Wimbledon, U.S. Open,
and Australian Open Champion

Billie Jean is a terrific example of the importance of positive energy. She has been so successful in her life as a player and coach because she possesses unending and contagious enthusiasm and determination. Billie's talent and work ethic made it a pleasure to coach her for the biggest event in tennis history, the Battle of the Sexes. She was able to beat Bobby Riggs in the Houston Astrodome thirty-five years ago because of her ability to turn stress into challenge. This book will inspire countless others to reexamine their attitude toward pressure.

–Dennis Van der Meer, Tennis Coach, King's
Coach at the Battle of the Sexes

The more I grow as a professional and as a woman, the more I appreciate the importance of Billie Jean King. Billie took on challenges that changed our world-she founded the women's professional tennis tour, created a union for female tennis players, lobbied for gender equity on college campuses, and at the same time kept a "day job" as the Number 1 tennis player in the world! I remain in awe and have complete respect for her commitment to the sport of tennis and the empowerment of women. Billie is one of the most heroic pioneers that I have encountered, and the success she has achieved in her life is proof that pressure is in fact a privilege.

–Venus Williams, Four-Time Wimbledon Champion,
Two-Time U.S. Open Champion

PRESSURE IS A PRIVILEGE

Lessons I've Learned
from Life and the
Battle of the Sexes

Billie Jean King

with Christine Brennan

Preface by
Holly Hunter

LifeTime Media, Inc.
New York

LifeTime Media, Inc.
352 Seventh Avenue
New York, NY 10001
212-631-7524
Visit our Web site at www.lifetimemedia.com

ISBN: 978-0-9816368-0-1
ISBN 10: 0-9816368-0-2

Library of Congress Control Number: 2008924243

Executive Editor: Karyn Gerhard, LifeTime Media
Designer: Roger Gorman, Reiner Design

LifeTime Media is a proud member of the Green Press Initiative. This book is printed on Rolland Opaque paper consisting of 30% post-consumer waste material. By using this paper, we have saved approximately 119 trees, 83 million BTUs of energy and over 10,000 pounds of dangerous greenhouse gases. At LifeTime Media, we are committed to the responsible use of our natural resources.

All LifeTime Media titles are available for special promotions, premiums, and bulk purchase. For more information, please contact the manager of our special sales department at 212-631-7524 or sales@lifetimemedia.com.

Printed in the United States of America
10 9 8 7 6 5 4 3 2 1

Contents

For my parents, Bill and Betty Moffitt, and
my brother, Randy "R.J." Moffitt, who gave me
the compass of my life;

for my friends Susan Williams, Carole Graebner, and
Jerry Cromwell, who pointed me in the right direction;

for my coaches Clyde Walker, Alice Marble,
Frank Brennan, Sr., Scotty Deeds, Dr. Joan Johnson, and
Mervyn Rose, who
helped get me to Number 1;

and

for the love of my life, Ilana Kloss, who gives me the
strength and support to keep living the dream.

Preface

We all have opportunities in our lives. Billie Jean King's talent brought her plenty—and when they came knocking on her door she already had a few plans. But she also creates her own opportunities, and has an inherent understanding of the responsibilities of them. Doors definitely opened for Billie and, in the case of her historic match against Bobby Riggs, she shook those doors off their hinges.

In 2001, I was honored to portray her in the made-for-television movie *When Billie Beat Bobby*. One of the biggest challenges of that role was that I didn't play tennis and I wanted to make sure that Billie never saw me hit a ball. But within hours of meeting her—not days, hours—Billie somehow talked me into going to a tennis court. I found myself facing her across the net. I was very scared. But she was unintimidating and persuasive and immediately helped me play better. I could not imagine how she could still be that close to beginner's tennis—to the psychological and physical mechanics of it. But Billie is the rare person who combines the gift of being an inspiring, instinctual teacher with being a brilliant and instinctual world-class performer. I understand why so many of the world's top tennis players have sought her advice to improve their games and their lives.

Billie Jean King is a global treasure. Few born leaders truly have the courage and stamina to live up to the responsibilities that come with the gifts they have been given. But, Billie has found a private strength by connecting with those responsibilities and she has architected a life that protects her and the fragile quality of her own humanity.

Billie has given all of us so much and, as she details in *Pressure Is a Privilege: Lessons I've Learned from Life and the Battle of the Sexes*, there is so much more we can learn from her. For more than forty years, society has put her on a pedestal and looked to her to break down the barriers that have challenged us. She has not disappointed. In fact she has reveled in the challenge. She is a philanthropist in the truest, most raw sense of the word. Her actions have nothing to do with money and everything to do with the virtue of the deed. She has always put herself in a position to fight the good fight.

And she never quits.

—Holly Hunter

....

Foreword

September 20, 1973. I was just starting my sophomore year in high school in the suburbs of Toledo, Ohio, when Billie Jean King played tennis hustler and self-declared male chauvinist Bobby Riggs in the "Battle of the Sexes." That was a very different time in our world. There were only three or four channels to pick from on the television dial, so when a big event was aired, the audience was huge and the impact was immediate. Billie Jean's win was an historic moment witnessed by millions of people at the same time. We all watched as history was made. In the course of just a few hours, the perception of women in the United States changed forever.

Billie Jean ruled women's tennis in the late 1960s and early 1970s with a demeanor on court that was a startling departure from that of the more demure women who preceded her. It was great to see a female athlete who was so aggressive. As a young player myself, I wore a tennis dress that looked like the kind King wore, sleeveless with a zipper up the middle and a big striped collar. I was so enthusiastic about the sport that my family took a small black-and-white television set on vacation to northern Michigan every year so I wouldn't miss Wimbledon.

Women's and girls' sports were very different in those days. Although I was the "tomboy" of the neighborhood, playing and watching sports with the boys for weeks on end, there were no organized teams for me to join until my freshman year of high school.

When I did get to play on a team, my experience was quite different from the boys'. Before field hockey games, we sometimes had to dash out and mow the grass on our field, then add the white lines. (Of course, the football field was in pristine condition three days before the next game.) We didn't have buses for our games and had to cancel softball games if we didn't have enough parents to drive us. And the cheerleaders for the boys' teams had better uniforms than we did.

This was the world of girls' and women's sports the day Billie Jean played Bobby. Our gym teacher and the coach of most of our girls' sports teams, Sandy Osterman, had us all worked up in the days leading to the match. In gym class and at our practices, if a boy came by, Miss O yelled out, "We know who's going to win the big match!" There were side bets worth all of a few dollars between Miss O and her male coaching counterparts. "We'll see who wins," she'd say with a mischievous laugh.

I finished my homework early to watch the match that night. It was a carnival atmosphere when Billie Jean and Bobby came on the court. Years later, when I got to know Billie, she told me that she had been extremely nervous. But I never knew. On television, she looked calm and confident.

Before the match started, my father and mother pointed out the subtlety behind Riggs's over-the-top bravado; while he was a blatant male chauvinist, they said he didn't seem to be a terrible guy. "He's acting bad, but in some ways, he's just playing along," my Dad said. "He's the perfect opponent for Billie Jean. He makes you want her to win even more."

As it was, I already wanted her to win very badly. Billie Jean was one of the very few female sports heroes I had. But there was no reason for me to worry that night. Billie Jean routed Bobby, 6-4, 6-3, 6-3, throwing her wood racket into the air as we cheered in the family room. It was the first time I had ever seen a woman beat a man at anything.

The next day at our lockers in the high school hallway, I spotted one of the star boy athletes in my grade, an athletic rival of mine who also was a good friend.

"We won," I said to him. "The girls won."

"Yeah, I know," he said, grimacing and walking away.

In the many years since, a few men have told me they thought it was one of the most over-hyped sports events of all time. I always disagree. "For you, maybe, but not for me," I tell them.

I have talked to Billie Jean quite a few times in interviews, at dinners, at Wimbledon, even at a White House dinner, where, nearly two decades into my career, she pulled me aside to get my thoughts on the women's sports movement. I smiled about that later: there was Billie Jean King asking me for my opinion on the topic that she pioneered and forever changed for the better.

No matter when or where we talk, I always make sure to thank Billie Jean for what she did that night in Houston. It is surely overkill by now, but I cannot help it.

"What you meant to a fifteen-year-old girl in Toledo, Ohio…" I tell her.

I never complete the sentence. She knows.

—Christine Brennan

Introduction

The night of September 20, 1973, was unique for the world. It was also the night that changed my life forever.

That evening more than 30,000 people came to the Astrodome in Houston, Texas, and millions more tuned in to ABC to watch an event that was labeled the "Battle of the Sexes."

It was a night that was part spectacle, part tennis match, part cultural phenomenon; a night when I entered the Astrodome on an Egyptian litter carried by four muscular men and my foil, the self-described male chauvinist Bobby Riggs, entered in a rickshaw pulled by a group of beautiful women (his "bosom buddies," as he called them).

It was also the night I ran Riggs all over the court and beat him in straight sets, 6-4, 6-3, 6-3.

If you are in your mid-forties or older, you probably remember watching the match, or at least hearing about it. If you are younger than that, you may have heard people speak about it. Even now, thirty-five years later, I am humbled by the thought that so many people not only watched the match but remember where they were when it happened, that it was such a significant event in their lives that it continues to influence them and remains prominent in their minds.

People have always asked me how this famous match came about, and how I came to play it. Let me give you a little history.

Bobby Riggs has been described as one of the top ten tennis players of all time through the Rod Laver era. In the late 1930s and 1940s he was at the top of his game and was ranked number one in the world in 1946 and 1947. When I was playing tennis in Southern California in the 1950s (where Riggs also grew up), I heard all about Bobby Riggs, the local tennis hero, and like everyone else I admired him.

Flash forward to the early 1970s. Watergate was heating up, Vietnam was cooling down, and the women's movement was at its peak. There were no fax machines, no microwaves, no cable television, and it was impossible for a woman to get her own credit card without a man as a co-signer.

Bobby was in his mid-fifties but was still acting like a kid. Still talented, still respected, he was also still an incurable hustler and motor-mouth. For years, whenever we were at the same event he would buzz around me like a little gnat, saying, "Play me! Play me!" I always told him I was too busy. And I really was! I had been an activist for women in sports nearly as long as I had *been* a woman in sports. I was also an activist for equal rights and opportunities for boys and girls, and women and men, in other areas of life. In the early 1970s, I was playing regularly while also working to get the women's professional tennis tour (then known as the Virginia Slims Series) started and helping to get Title IX—the groundbreaking legislation that would require all high schools, colleges, and universities receiving federal funds for education to spend those funds equally on boys and girls—passed in Congress. (It was eventually passed on June 23, 1972, about a year before the Battle of the Sexes.) With traveling, playing tournaments, giving interviews, owning a small business, doing promotions for the Virginia Slims series, and a thousand other things that filled my days, my time was stretched thin enough as it was; there was no way I could squeeze in the training and preparation I would need to play Bobby. So my answer was always "No."

I did not want anything to set back the struggle that I and so many other women were enduring, and I wondered what would happen if I—or any other woman— lost to Bobby. Everything was unsettled in women's sports, and a loss to Riggs (or any man) could have reinforced the many arguments against us. So over and over I told Bobby I would not play him. He finally stopped asking, but his mania to play a Battle of the Sexes match did not go away.

Since I would not bite, Riggs went next to Chris Evert's father, Jimmy (Chris was not even twenty and already an acclaimed player), who declined on Chris's behalf, and then to Margaret Court (Margaret finished 1973 as the top-ranked female player in the world). He was able to convince Margaret to play a televised match to see who was better. But it was not just about who was better between Bobby and Margaret—it was about whether men or women were better. I remember being in Detroit for the Virginia Slims tournament and riding in an elevator with Margaret when she told me about the match. I said to her, "Do you understand what this is about? This isn't just about tennis. This is about social change, about women's sports and women's rights."

Margaret was excited about the $35,000 payday (and who wouldn't have been?). I am not really sure what she was thinking, but I was concerned that she might not truly understand the repercussions in the United States or on Title IX that playing Bobby in 1973 could have, or that the match was more about women's equality than about putting on an exhibition.

The Riggs/Court match was televised on Mother's Day, May 13, 1973. Unfortunately I was not able to be at the match itself; I was at a tournament in Japan. As I boarded the plane back to the States, I asked a flight attendant if anyone knew what happened in the match. I could not believe what I heard—Bobby had won, 6-2, 6-1. I found out later that he beat Margaret in a scant 57 minutes. The match quickly became known as the "Mother's Day Massacre."

I actually didn't get to see the match until the night before my own match with Bobby. I sat down to watch the tape, and before the match even started, disaster struck. When Margaret walked onto the court, Bobby gave her roses and she curtsied as she received them from him. Yes, she *curtsied.* With that one little gesture, it was clear the match was already over.

When Margaret lost, I immediately knew what I had to do: I had no choice—I had to play Bobby, and I had to beat him. I was a women's libber—or, as Gladys Heldman, the publisher of *World Tennis* magazine, nicknamed female tennis players, women's "lobbers"— and I was perceived as one of the leaders of the women's sports movement, a role I had accepted. Though I had resisted before, playing Bobby in the wake of Margaret's televised defeat now became a critical move to regain footing and take the lead for women's equality, on and off the tennis court. So when Bobby again asked me to play him, I accepted the challenge. But I looked him straight in the eye and said, "Bobby, this is a one-shot deal. I will play you this time, but I will never play you again, no matter what you do or how much money you offer."

Our Battle of the Sexes was announced on July 11, 1973 and was set up to be played on September 20, 1973—four months after the Riggs/Court match.

The match was winner-take-all, and the $100,000 prize money was the largest amount paid to date for a single tennis match. The build-up to it was immense. It was hyped on every television station, in newspapers, and in magazines for weeks before the event; we were interviewed relentlessly and the press conferences after every match I played were flooded by media from all over the country, asking me questions about the upcoming match; and I was constantly stopped by people on the street who wanted to talk about it. (I think the press was a bit surprised to hear me say that I was not playing the game to prove that women could beat men. I told them I never thought women were better than men, and that the top man in tennis would beat the top woman. I was playing to prove that men and women had the same entertainment value, which is why we should be paid equally. But in the maelstrom of the "battle of the sexes" hype, all of that got swept under the carpet.) The stakes were high, and the media pressure made them even higher. If I lost, it was going to be an even bigger blow for women's rights than Margaret's loss had been—Bobby would now have proved his point by beating not one but two of the top-ranked women in the sport.

The amount of preparation I put into the match was different than other matches. First of all, I had never played a five-set match (women's tennis matches were—and still are—best two out of three sets), so not only did I have to be in "match shape," I had to make sure I was able to go the distance. Also, I knew the adrenaline was going to be higher and the emotion deeper in this match than in any other of my career. I had to be prepared to handle the experience so I could remain calm on the court. But the most important issue for me was that, unlike other matches where a re-match was possible, the match against Bobby was a one-time, all-or-nothing deal.

That momentous night, the telecast appropriately began with the glib tune "Anything You Can Do, I Can Do Better." ABC played the gender angle to the hilt, and why not? It was a great story line. It tapped into a timely and heated issue for sports, education, and business; the gender equality issue at its peak had stirred controversy in every aspect of American life. Few things could have attracted as much buzz.

Even the celebrities had come out to be a part of the incredible energy, the electric charge of the occasion. Andy Williams was spotted in the crowd. So were Lee Majors, Farrah Fawcett, JoAnn Pflug, Blythe Danner, and Glenn Campbell. It was so unusual: A tennis match unfolding just like the big heavyweight fight nights used to. (Speaking of heavyweights, George Foreman picked me to win; NFL great Jim Brown picked Bobby.)

Up in the broadcast booth, ABC announcer Howard

Cosell brought it all to life. "Bobby has talked so much that there is unquestionably an overwhelming sentiment for Billie Jean King," he said in that familiar nasal voice. "You can hear the roar."

As four track and field stars from Rice University carried me to my spot on the court, Cosell said, "Here comes Billie Jean King—a very attractive young lady; if she ever let her hair grow down to her shoulders and took her glasses off, you'd have someone vying for a Hollywood screen test." I appreciated the compliment, but he barely mentioned my accomplishments as an athlete. Though the man-versus-woman angle was understandably being played up, that kind of sexism was still over the top, especially for an announcer as he was introducing me.

Ah, 1973.

Down on the court, it was an absolute circus—there was a marching band, majorettes doing a kick-line, and hundreds of people swarming around the litter as I was brought in. In the stands, thousands of people were screaming and applauding, some holding signs (one man had a sign around his neck that said, inexplicably, "Billie wears jockey shorts"), but to me it was all a big blur. In fact, the only person I remember seeing while up on that litter was Pam Austin, Tracy Austin's older sister and a fellow player on the Virginia Slims Series, holding a sign that said "Bye" (part of a set of signs that read "Bye Bye Bobby"). She was the one familiar face I could find, so I zeroed in on her. I waved and said "Hi" before turning back to the crowd swarming around me, and focusing on the match (even though I couldn't see the court because of all the people).

Bobby had his own melee going on. He was brought into the statium on a rickshaw pulled by his "bosom buddies." Ever the promoter, Bobby came onto the court wearing a yellow warm-up jacket with the Sugar Daddy logo (his well-chosen sponsor for the match) splashed all over it.

It was big-time television, so before the match started we had a little showboating to do. Picking up a gigantic Sugar Daddy lollipop, Bobby said over the loudspeaker, "Billie Jean is going to be a sucker for my wiles tonight, so I brought her the biggest sucker I could find." I then turned around and presented him with his own "chauvinist pig"—a live piglet, complete with a big pink bow.

Finally, it was time for the match to start. I waited for Bobby to take off the warm-up jacket, but he didn't. We started the match with the Sugar Daddy logo glaring in my face. "Bobby's being paid too much money to take that off," said ABC commentator Rosie Casals, a colleague and friend of mine. I loved that she said that.

The match got off to a shaky start. Bobby and I were both nervous and making uncharacteristic mistakes; it was nerve-wracking playing in front of a crowd that large in a gigantic stadium that was in no way designed to host a tennis match. If we hit a lob, the ball was completely lost in the glare of the lights and the ceiling, which seemed a mile high and bright white.

I had to win the first set if I was going to win the match. I needed the psychological advantage. We both held serve, and Bobby finally took off the jacket after the third game of the first set when he was behind, 2-1. Howard Cosell said probably the best line of the night: "There goes Bobby with the jacket off and maybe the braggadocio a little bit reduced."

In the fourth game Bobby held serve and evened the match at 2-2. In the fifth game, Bobby broke my serve, and before I knew it I was down 2-3. It was my moment of truth—I had to regain control. Bobby's technique was to put a lot of spin on the ball and not much behind it, which meant that I would have to supply all of the power. But I decided to put it back on him by hitting the ball softly and all over the court; that way he would get worn out having to create all of the power and chasing after the ball. It worked like a charm; within minutes he was covered in sweat.

My confidence was up, but I knew I had a long, long way to go. As Yogi Berra said, "It ain't over 'til it's over." My adrenaline was pumping at high speed, but with the extended time between games (two minutes instead of the usual one) and sets (four minutes), the match seemed to be moving at an excruciatingly slow and arduous pace. I was worried about keeping my energy up if we ended up going all five sets. But I forced myself to stay in the moment and just focus on one ball at a time; it was the only way for me to get through it.

Before the match, ABC had asked Bobby and me to be interviewed between sets. I was hesitant; Bobby, of course, enthusiastically agreed. After the first set I knew I needed to stay focused, so I decided not to do the interview. But there was Bobby, chatting up Frank Gifford, the courtside commentator. I did talk to Frank after the second set, but by that point the match was such a blur, I have no idea what I said!

With the exception of spasms in my calves in the third set; the rest of the match went more easily than I could have hoped—until match point. I was up 5-3, but each time I was at match point, I completely choked. On my second match point, I recall hitting a forehand so low it hit the bar at the bottom of the net—how tight was I! I thought to myself, when I get the next match point I am going to put the ball so high over the net that he has to hit it—which is what I did. By then Bobby was so tired he put the ball in the net.

It was finally over. I had done it.

The relief of winning was huge. I tossed my wood racket into the air and Bobby jumped over the net to congratulate me. Even though we had a rivalry on the court, we truly did like each other. Now proven athletic peers as well as friends, we walked off the court arm in arm.

No matter how many matches I won in my long career, the Battle of the Sexes stands out not only for its fame, but also for its instructiveness. That match taught me more than I could have ever believed. I learned about pressure and how to handle it, about the right kind of preparation, about committment, about trusting my instincts, about friends, people, relationships, about finances, and perspective. I also learned about the importance of having a sense of humor and how to smile and laugh at myself, even in the most difficult moments.

The match also brought into action every lesson I had

been taught by my family, coaches, and friends; everything in my past was a building block that supported me as I set foot on that court with courage and conviction—especially the lesson of bringing all of myself to everything I do.

In the years since the Battle of the Sexes match, I have come to realize that the lessons I brought to it and learned from it are not exclusive to tennis. I have used these lessons in every aspect of my life, both business and personal. They are the tenets that have grounded me and given me the opportunity to lead a life that has been more fulfilling than I could have ever hoped.

I am a firm believer that each generation should help the next, and so I would like to share what I have learned with you. It is my hope that these life lessons will be as useful for you in your daily life as they have been for me. It is so important to have peace and harmony in your life and to be good to yourself. So if anything in these pages helps you live your life better, be happier, be more productive in your job, or be a better parent, neighbor, or friend, then this book will have been a success. I hope you enjoy reading *Pressure Is a Privilege*. Go for it!

Chapter One

Relationships are Everything

You know about the most famous person in my life: Bobby Riggs. But well before he showed up, there was Susan Williams.

If you said, "Who on earth is she?" you're not alone. Susan's dad worked for Shell Chemical and in 1954 got transferred to California, which led to her family moving to Long Beach and to her sitting next to me in Mrs. Delph's fifth grade class. Susan was a brilliant girl and one of my closest friends, but that was not the only reason she was important in my life. One day in class, she asked me:

"Do you want to play tennis?"

A simple question, but one that would have a profound impact on me.

"What's tennis?" I replied.

"You get to run, jump and hit a ball," Susan said.

Those were my three most favorite things to do, so I said, "Sure, I'll try it!"

I did not come from a tennis-playing family. We were all athletic—my father played basketball, mom was a great body-surfer, they both loved dancing, and my brother and I both loved playing team sports—but tennis was not on our radar. In the 1950s and 1960s, it was still perceived as a country-club sport, and we definitely were not a country-club family.

But Susan's family was, so that weekend I found myself heading out with Susan to try this new sport—at their country club, of course. I walked onto the gray cement courts of the Virginia Country Club wearing a pair of white shorts my mother had sewn for me and carrying a racket loaned to me by Susan. That first day, Susan taught me to drop the ball, let it bounce, then hit it. I didn't know what I was doing, but we had a great time hitting (with me whiffing a few, probably) balls all over the court.

That was my first time playing tennis, but it was not my epiphany moment. I liked the sport, but I had not yet fallen in love. Sometimes you do not quite recognize that you have found your life's work, especially when you are approaching the ripe old age of eleven! Besides, even at that age I knew that if I could only play tennis at the country club, there was little chance of me playing it on a regular basis. So it was just one more sport to enjoy with my new friend whenever we could play it.

A few weeks later, Susan and I were playing softball at Houghton Park in Long Beach when Val Halloran, our coach, told us about a nice gentleman who gave free tennis lessons at the park every Tuesday. Tennis—free! That was all I needed to hear. The next Tuesday, Susan and I went to the park, excited at the chance to play together more regularly. Besides, Susan was the best young player in Long Beach, as far as I was concerned, so I had a long way to go to catch up with her.

Clyde Walker changed everything. He was the "nice gentleman," the tennis instructor for the Parks and Recreation department in Long Beach. The first lesson he taught us was to close the gate! He immediately intrigued me and he made me laugh. I had enjoyed learning the basics of hitting a tennis ball around with Susan, but in the span of a couple of hours Clyde made tennis come alive—he made it FUN. The other children and I laughed and ran around practicing the game-like drills he taught us. With Clyde as a coach it was a delight to learn how to hold the racquet, how to hit the ball, and how to run to a shot.

That was it. That first Tuesday afternoon, I was hooked.

When my mother came to pick me up after my first group lesson with Clyde Walker, in Houghton public park, I immediately told her I knew what I was going to do with my life—I was going to be the number one tennis player in the world. And I meant it.

Resourcefulness will get you far in life, and here is a perfect example. My parents were happy to see me so excited, but they told me that if I wanted a racket, I would have to buy it. I was only eleven and didn't have a job. So, without a cent to my name, I had to come up with an idea. And I did. I decided that I would go to some of our neighbors looking for work! Although they chuckled when I approached them with my idea, most of them indulged me by creating odd jobs in and around their homes. They paid me to take out trash, tidy up gardens—anything they asked me to do, I did. I took advantage of every opportunity and pretty soon I had $8.29 saved in a Mason jar.

I had no idea if it would be enough, but I just could not wait any longer, so I asked my parents to take me to Brown's Sporting Goods. The salesperson asked me what kind of racket I wanted; I held out the money from my jar and asked, "What will $8.29 buy?" The answer was a wood racquet with purple strings, white throat, and a purple grip, which I bought happily because purple was my favorite color.

And thus a tennis career was born.

Every person's life contains an endless number of possible turning points—usually a moment where an opportunity is presented to you or what someone says or does affects a choice you have to make. I think everyone has met at least one person who created a turning point for them. Muhammad Ali and I used to talk about this concept a lot. Because his career and mine ran pretty parallel in the 1960s and 70s, we ended up going to many of the same banquets and luncheons. We would sit next to each other and talk about the fact that you never know how another person is going to touch your life, or how you are going to touch his or hers, and how important it is to keep yourself open.

Sometimes you don't even recognize the critical moment until much later. Still, it is important to try to be aware. Practicing awareness is an ongoing process for all of us. In fact, there have been times when I have almost missed out on an amazing opportunity because

Muhammad Ali and I had a genuine affection for each other. Whenever we would run into each other, he would whisper in my ear, "Billie Jean King, you're the queen." I have no idea know how much he thought about how our struggles for recognition as athletes ran parallel, but I think it was definitely a part of our connection. We were fighting the same fight in different ways, as pro athletes trying to even the playing field for minorities. And yet, I think we were both very focused on trying to improve the world for everyone.

I was distracted. For instance: About two weeks before the King/Riggs match, Jerry Perenchio, the promoter of the event, invited me to a party he was hosting in Los Angeles. I almost didn't go—I was in the middle of training for the match and was just not in a party mood. But I went anyway, and when I got there, I asked Jerry why he was having the party. He told me the party was for Elton John. I almost fainted. Elton was—and still is—my favorite musician.

I was so nervous and shy that I could not get up the courage to talk to Elton, so we spent the whole party on opposite sides of the room. The party was almost over before Tony King, one of Elton's staff members, approached me and asked if he could introduce me to Elton. I nervously said yes. Because of his passion for sports and my passion for music (I think most athletes secretly want to be musicians and most musicians secretly want to be athletes!), Elton and I hit it off immediately. We talked about our shyness and realized that both of us had been too shy to make the first move. We only got to talk for about thirty seconds, and I thought we would never meet again—we hadn't even exchanged phone numbers.

The following year, in 1974, I returned to London for Wimbledon. When I checked into the hotel there was a message waiting for me. I have no idea how he did it, but somehow Elton found out I was staying at the Gloucester Hotel and had left a message for me to call him. I returned the call; he wanted to get together. I asked him when, and he said, "What are you doing now?" I was free, so he came over immediately after we hung up. We sat in his Rolls Royce outside the Gloucester, listening to his music on the car's twenty-eight-speaker sound system, and talked for hours. A lifelong friendship was born.

Later that summer, Elton joined us as our "unofficial cheerleader" for the World TeamTennis team, the

Philadelphia Freedoms. He was a big part of our team—he sat on the bench with us, and I even took him to Ted Tinling, who had designed our uniforms, to be fitted for one of the red, white, and blue uniforms. One night he told me he wanted to write a song for me. Sure enough, in August of that year, during the first match of the World TeamTennis play-offs at the old Denver Auditorium Arena, Elton brought me a rough mix of "Philadelphia Freedom" that he and Bernie Taupin had written and recorded during the Caribou sessions in Colorado. He played the new song for me and my teammates in the locker room. I was blown away.

"Philadelphia Freedom" ended up hitting Number 1 on the pop charts and became Elton's first crossover hit, topping the R & B charts as well. Thank goodness for Jerry Perenchio, thank goodness for Tony King, and thank goodness I went to that party!

Of course, all of these people—Susan Williams, Clyde Walker, Val Halloran, Muhammad Ali, and Elton John—were people who touched my life in a positive way, but we can be just as deeply influenced by people who have the potential to be a negative influence. The key is to turn those negative influences into positive ones. These people can show us what we *don't* want to be; they serve as reminders of the roads we do not want to travel.

Remember, too, that the people who will influence our lives may not always be people you meet face to face. For instance, some of today's athletes who are cheating by taking performance-enhancing drugs come to mind as negative influences on the lives of their fans, family and friends, and especially on the lives of those children who see them as heroes and want to emulate them. The same is true for politicians who are found to be dishonest. Theirs are cautionary tales, useful in helping to teach children how *not* to conduct their lives.

Every person we meet has the potential to be somebody influential in our lives. Were it not for Susan, I am sure I never would have been introduced to tennis; I wouldn't have been interested in the free lessons in the park; and obviously I never would have come to play Bobby Riggs. That might sound dramatic, but it's true. All these years later, I still find myself saying thank goodness Susan's family moved to Long Beach, thank goodness she sat next to me in school, thank goodness she asked me to play, and thank goodness I tried it— not to mention, thank goodness for Val Halloran, for free lessons in the park, and for Clyde Walker. All these random meetings came together like pieces of a jigsaw puzzle in just the right way to make me who I am today.

We never know what's going to happen next or what side roads will be discovered. So it is good to always have your mind open, ready to meet the next person on your journey. I believe in being aware, being open to opportunities, and *listening*. We can learn something from everyone, no matter who it is or what the situation.

In my case, all it took was a simple "Yes" in fifth grade, and I was on my way.

INSTANT REPLAY

Relationships are Everything

We cannot predict how or when someone is going to touch our life in a way that will change it forever. Take advantage of every opportunity, try everything, and always stay alert. Doors—some invisible, some big and boldly painted—will constantly be set in front of us, but it is up to you to open them and step through.

Chapter Two

Lessons at the Dinner Table

I was lucky to be born into a loving family who helped shape me into the person I am today. Let me take you back to our middle-class home in Long Beach, California, in the 1950s.

My parents were married in a Methodist church. Both from families of divorce, they were very committed to unity and to the idea of a strongly bonded family. This joint dedication, along with their personal values, gave my brother and me a very supportive foundation for our sports careers and for our lives.

My father was a firefighter and a Navy man. As you can imagine, this meant a pretty strict household—and he had a bit of a temper. I remember once getting a C in chemistry class, and he told me he wouldn't let me play tennis for two months (but he felt bad about the punishment and gave in after two weeks). My dad may have set firm boundaries, but he was also a soft touch, and he always did everything he could for us. His parents were divorced when he was only thirteen years old, so having a solid, stable family was important to him. And even though dad took a pretty hard line, and was more unpredictable than my mom, he had his fun side, too—he loved to tell jokes, and he was a jock, basketball being his favorite sport. My dad actually played against the legendary Jackie Robinson while in junior college and later played basketball in the Navy. He was so good that the NBA tapped him for a tryout. He declined the invitation—I had already been born, and to my father being a family man meant providing security, so he opted for a job with a regular paycheck and good benefits. But I think the experience helped him to understand my own dreams of success in sports. I always felt that he really got me.

Although she liked sports and being active, my mother was not as wrapped up in all of it as the rest of us. My mother was a pretty traditional 1950s homemaker and was fantastic with her hands, always crocheting, knitting, and sewing. She was also big on perseverance and seeing things through—I sometimes jokingly call her the "velvet hammer" because she was quiet but she never let up until the job was finished. For example, when I was a child I desperately wanted to play piano. It took my parents five years to save up for a piano (a great lesson in delayed gratification!), and once we got it I played all the time. Then tennis came into my life. I wanted to give up the piano, but my mother would not let me until I could read music. For her, it was important to *finish*, not quit.

My brother Randy (my family and I called him R.J., which he preferred) shared our father's love for sports, but his dedication was to baseball. When we were little, R.J. and I would play catch together for hours. We did not have much of a back yard, so like most kids in the neighborhood we played out in the streets. It was something we enjoyed until he turned twelve—by then, his arm had gotten so strong that it hurt my hand to catch his throws! We still played other games together, like hide and seek, and we walked to school together every day until I reached seventh grade. (We went to different schools then, and I really missed him.) We even got seriously involved in sports—tennis for me, baseball for him—at about the same time, which was difficult for our parents since it kept them running from practice to match to game. Eventually, R.J. fulfilled his dream of becoming a major league baseball player, playing more than ten years in the majors (as Randy Moffitt), mostly as a right-handed relief pitcher with the San Francisco Giants; he also played for the Houston Astros and ended his career with the Toronto Blue Jays (he had a great slider).

My dad worked a schedule that was twenty-four hours on and twenty-four hours off, so with his odd hours and all of our sports and other activities, it was hard to find us all in one place at the same time—except for dinner. R.J. and I had to be home on time for dinner every night at 5:15 pm or we would be in trouble. I cannot tell you how many times my brother and I ran like maniacs to make sure we made it to the table on time! On days when dad worked a twenty-four-hour work shift, R.J. and I ate with mom. But whether it was just mom and us or the entire family, we all had dinner together with no distractions allowed: no television or phones (obviously there were no cell phones or PDAs to bring to the dinner table back then). Not many families do this anymore.

Dinner was a time for us to just sit down and talk, to connect, check in and find out what we were up to, air grievances, laugh, and tell stories. My parents would talk to us about school, sports, our problems, even things like philosophy. I remember once my father asking us what we thought was the most important thing in life (my father thought it was peace of mind; my mother thought it was "to thine own self be true;" R.J. and I thought it was the golden rule—treating others the way you would want them to treat you).

We not only talked to our parents, we learned from them. My parents have been a huge influence on my life. Having two children wrapped up in competitive sports at such early ages meant that they missed out a little on enjoying our childhood. I remember once my mother told me how much she missed me, and my dad said, "You have to let her go pursue her dream." Still, they were always very proud of R.J. and me. And they were very big on instilling good values in us from a very early age. Most of those lessons were taught right there at the dinner table. The lessons were not profound or earth-shattering, but they were—and still are—absolutely essential. People are wonderfully kind to acknowledge all the work I have done on behalf of gender equality and other social issues, but the truth is that everything I have done in my adult life has stemmed from or was influenced by those very basic lessons I learned around the dinner table in Long Beach.

We were not allowed to swear in our house—in fact, we were not even allowed to use slang—it wasn't, "Yeah," it was, "Yes." Every request was followed by a "please," every kind action, a "thank you." This was not just a rule for the children; my parents practiced this as well. And respecting others works just as well in the corporate boardroom as it did at our house. If someone is about to spend money on one of our projects, or to pay me to be a spokesperson, or to be a sponsor of

My rival and good friend Chris Evert and I spent a lot of time over the years talking about our families. We have been amazed to find out we were brought up similarly with many of the same values. I suppose that is not so strange among adults raised during the 1950s and 60s, but these values are not something you hear people talking a lot about anymore. It has been a nice point of connection for Chris and me.

One day at the French Open in 1981 she and I were talking as usual. I mentioned that, when I was a child, I participated in Youth for Christ at my school and read my

Bible every night at bedtime. I also told her that at one point in my childhood I wanted to be a missionary. She started to laugh, and I felt a little embarrassed. I thought that maybe the idea of me being a missionary sounded silly. But she was not laughing at me at all. "I once wanted to be a missionary, too!," she said. Many young people who are passionate about helping others or creating social change may consider religious work as a possible venue, especially if they are raised in church-going families. It was nice to hear a contemporary of mine share that she felt the same way and to know that similar childhood urges can end up driving two different women to each do her share in different ways as an adult.

World TeamTennis, the co-ed tennis league I co-founded, I think they feel better about our arrangement because of the polite, respectful tone at the table.

Even though our family tried to be polite and respectful, it doesn't mean we always were. In fact, often we would talk over each other at our home! To this day I am still trying to be better about interrupting others. This is one of the things I will be working on for the rest of my life. But I *will* keep working on it. After so many years negotiating, dealing with politics, and otherwise just building relationships with people of all types in all kinds of circumstances, I know the little things can make a big difference.

For my parents, part of respecting others meant listening to my elders. I have to admit, this one was easy for me. I have always been fascinated by the older generation, even as a child. I adored learning about their lives, listening to their opinions, anything they wanted to share with me. When I began playing tennis, I would always ask older, more experienced players about their matches, what brought them to tennis, and what they thought was important. Listening to our elders can be very rewarding, not to mention fascinating and fun. It's something that I don't think enough young people take advantage of—today's culture seems to only focus on the ills of aging instead of the wisdom it can bring. I certainly wouldn't have learned how to play a great game of tennis had I not listened to my elders.

My family also taught me the importance of giving to those less fortunate than myself. My parents were committed to helping others. They had lived through the hardships of the Great Depression and World War II, and never had anything handed to them. But no matter how bad it got, they knew that there were always people worse off than they were, and whatever they could do to help, they did. My parents supported the Salvation Army and veteran's associations and really believed in the importance of community organizations. Seeing their generosity and how it affected others had a tremendous impact on me. I am always pleased when I hear about a corporation giving back, or helping in the community, especially when the shareholders have a say in where the funds go. Over the years, I have become involved with a number of charities, including the Women's Sports Foundation and the Elton John AIDS Foundation. It is one of my true passions. My parents used to say, "To whom much is given, much is required." True, it comes from the Bible, but I also heard it at our kitchen table. And half a century later, I still believe the better off you are, the more you need to help others who are less fortunate.

Similarly, the memory of my parents' example always reminds me to be thankful for what I have. This carries over to my job as a role model or as an example or whatever you want to call me, and I take it very seriously. Every person I sign an autograph for deserves my respect and thanks. Every underserved child I meet at a tennis clinic deserves the same attention as a CEO. But gratitude needs to be on a personal level as well. I think it's so important to show the people around us how much we appreciate them.

These lessons are the cornerstone of who I am, and learning them gave me confidence to create the life I have today. They are my equilibrium and my balance; they are the rudder of my ship, the things that keep me on course. I would not be the person I am if my parents had not instilled these lessons in me.

Not everyone is blessed with a close-knit family or with strong parental role models, and every family has challenges. It would be too Pollyanna-ish of me to think that wasn't the case! But even if you didn't have a positive environment growing up, it is still possible to have similar touchstones in your life. Loved ones, friends, teachers, professors, or colleagues—these can be the people at your dinner table. Everyone needs at least one person who loves them unconditionally and believe in them.

These lessons may seem old-fashioned, or just like a plain cliché, but I really believe it's important to remind ourselves of them every once in a while. As I go through life, it seems more and more that our society doesn't place as much value on these "golden rules" as it once did. I see so many people who either were not taught them or maybe just forgot them, which is a shame. Reminding ourselves of these simple, yet powerful rules can not only make our own lives better, but they can also improve the world for everyone. And isn't that the point of a fulfilling life?

INSTANT REPLAY

Five Rules for Life:
From My Dinner Table to Yours

Be polite.

Show respect to yourself and others.

Listen to and engage your elders.

Give to those less fortunate than yourself.

Show gratitude.

Chapter Three

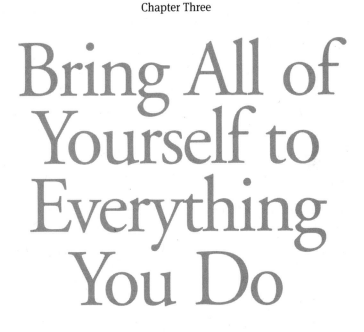

Bring All of Yourself to Everything You Do

Holly Hunter played me in *When Billie Beat Bobby*, the movie about the Battle of the Sexes, and we became great friends during filming. Holly and her partner, actor Gordon McDonald, attended the renaming ceremony for the USTA National Tennis Center in New York on August 28, 2006. While they were in town, my partner, Ilana, and I had dinner with them a few days later. In the course of the conversation, Holly said, "Billie, I love that you bring all of yourself to everything you do." She was very sweet to say that about me, but she lives this way every day of her life.

I had never heard it put in such a great way! Bringing

all of myself is one of my main codes of life. I'm a per-fectioniste—if I do something, I do it all out. It doesn't matter if I'm playing tennis, giving a speech, doing an interview, working for my favorite presidential candi-date, shooting a commercial, or simply seeing a friend; I commit myself and live my life to the fullest. And it's not always with things that people might perceive as "active"—when I meditate, I also bring all of myself. I relax deeply. I focus on my breathing. I embrace the moment. And because I do that, I get the most benefit out of my meditation time.

Everyone approaches life differently—some people are aggressive and boisterous, others are quiet and intro-

Being a perfectionist is actually a weakness and a strength for me. When I was holding up the Wimbledon plate I was already thinking about what I could do better at my next match. I do the same thing in our offices—if you ask my co-workers, they'll say I'm a maniac! It is something I have to work on.

Be sure to give yourself enough time to enjoy your vic-tories—they are part of what make life wonderful!

spective. But no matter how we approach life, completely committing ourselves to whatever we do is essential. It often means the difference between success and disappointment, the difference between doing an okay job and doing a great job. If you have committed yourself, you have given it your best shot, and that's all you can do.

Though I played many incredible matches, the Battle of the Sexes was one of the biggest events of my career, and one of the most important symbolic events in the advancement of women in our culture and in sports. I was aware of its significance at the time, but in order to win I had to remain focused on the immediate goal: I just wanted to beat Bobby Riggs. So I totally embraced the opportunity.

Preparation is the key to "bringing" all of myself. When match day arrives, it is already too late. Some players just get by with saving their all for the match and holding back during practice times, but champions don't. They bring all of themselves to practice so that they can bring all of themselves to the match. If you do not practice with the same intensity that you plan to bring to the match or any important event— what we call "match play"—you can undermine your performance. Putting all that effort into the preparation—not the day before, but weeks or even months before—also means that when the critical moment arrives, you can relax and enjoy yourself, knowing that you are ready. Getting ready emotionally, physically, mentally, and spiritually puts me in a position to win, and the Riggs match was no different—I knew if I didn't prepare specifically for this match, I would be in trouble. So I did absolutely everything I could to get ready.

Emotional preparation was the first step, so before I even said yes to Bobby, I did some major-league soul searching. I thought about all of the possible scenarios and outcomes and all of the pros and cons of playing the match. I studied it like I study tennis itself. I wanted to make sure I understood every aspect of what I was getting myself into. I asked myself, "Can I afford to lose this match? What are the consequences? What would happen if I got injured prior to the match? What would happen if I got sick?"

The pros were simple: If I won, it might get the minds and hearts of Americans to begin to match up on issues of equality, and, I hoped, create real support for Title IX. People had heard about these issues, and now, if I took on Bobby, they would see them play out on the court.

Another pro was that people who had never watched

tennis before would be watching our match—a match played by a woman and a man, and on prime-time television, no less (tennis had never been shown in prime time before). Though I am often thought of as an activist for women's tennis, I consider myself an activist for the sport at large. When I started playing tennis it was not on the general public's radar. Tennis was primarily a "country-club sport." But for my match against Bobby, the audience projections were huge—50 million people were expected to watch the match on television. Tennis was only dreaming of that kind of exposure in the 1970s, so I recognized that it was an incredible opportunity for women's tennis and also for the sport itself.

But the real pro, the one that ultimately outweighed the rest, was the chance to effect social change. If I could win, it would be a visual statement—a strong one.

The cons were pretty scary. First, though every match engenders a certain amount of intensity and stress, there is nothing as stressful as knowing you have only one shot. And this match against Bobby would be a one time deal. All or nothing. That is a lot of pressure!

I was painfully aware that if I lost, it could set women's sports and women's rights issues back significantly. And I didn't want anything to happen that would weaken the support for Title IX we had already fought so hard to win. I did not want to add fuel to the argument that we women did not deserve the improvements we were getting in education and athletics.

Also, on the con side, I was really concerned about what people would think if I lost. To beat someone who was literally as old as my father (Riggs was born in the same year as my dad), well, that wasn't a very big athletic feat in my mind. So I was a little nervous about how badly a loss would be perceived.

On a personal level—which was last on my list of things to think about—I was scared to death that, if I lost, I would be remembered as "the woman who lost to Bobby Riggs." Think about it: this match was probably the most exposure I was ever going to get in my life. It would have been a terrible time to choke. It is possible that none of my other achievements would matter in the shadow of this one defeat.

But you know what? I got over all that. I had to. Some people thought Bobby would demolish me as he had done with Margaret Court. All I had to do to banish my fears was to remind myself that I deserved to be there and that I would show them they were wrong to underestimate any woman.

After I did all of that emotional preparation and accepted Bobby's challenge, my next step was visualization. I imagined what would happen if I won. (I must admit, I liked that vision.) Then I imagined what it would be like to lose, and I got sick to my stomach. There is no doubt about it—the thought of defeat is a great incentive. Once I decided to put all of my efforts into winning and not even let the idea of losing enter my mind, I felt much better about everything.

The next step in the process was the physical, including training with weights (which was not anything like what we do today) and going to Shipyard Racquet Club in Hilton Head, South Carolina, to hit hundreds of overheads every day with teaching pro Pete Collins. I also talked with my coach, Frank Brennan, Sr., many times, and with Dennis Van der Meer, Margaret Court's coach. Dennis had attended Margaret's match against Bobby, so he had some specific strategic ideas for me.

Finally, I did my mental preparation, and a big piece of that was to get acclimated to the surroundings. I took a tour of the Astrodome the day before the match. (Few people remember—or realize—the week of King/Riggs I was still playing in a Virginia Slims tournament in Houston for Gladys Heldman, and so my mental and physical preparation for the Astrodome was all the more difficult.) It was important to me to know everything about the place so that there would be no surprises. I wanted to see what the fans would be seeing, where the court would be positioned in that cavernous arena, how high the ceiling was (plenty high, it turned out, even for the highest rain-maker lob), where the limo would drop me off, where the locker room was, which security guards I would have around me, who was going to be with me, and what they were like as people.

Walking into the arena's playing area was an eye-opener—it was unlike any other venue I'd played in or have played in since. Nothing in my career had prepared me for the vastness of the building, and the court itself didn't have the intimate environment or the symmetry of many of the venues where we played. Another issue was the court itself, which neither Bobby nor I got to practice on until the afternoon of the match. Sportease—a thin, smooth, carpet-like surface—had been rolled out on top of a basketball court, which made the playing surface dead and kept the ball low.

About two months before the match, I was very anxious. But because of all of the focused preparation I did, the closer the match got, the calmer I became. In fact, I was at such complete peace with everything that I decided to make an appearance at a sponsor's cocktail party in the upstairs bar area of the Astrodome about twenty minutes before the match to thank all those who had helped me get to that point. I have been told people were shocked by that gesture. But I knew I was ready, so why not be sociable? (And no, I did not have anything to drink—other than water.)

Once the match started and we were on the court, I didn't look out or allow myself to be distracted. I had gotten my entire mind, body, and soul ready for this match and I was completely present, using all of my senses. I spent the first few games feeling my way through things, then I stepped back for a moment, remembered all of my preparation, remembered to pay great attention and remain focused and relaxed, and took control of the match. From that moment on, I stayed in the now, played one ball at a time, and Bobby never regained the upper hand.

After proper preparation, how can we bring all of ourselves to whatever we do? First and foremost, I try to keep moving forward and I take things one step at a time. During the sixth game of the first set of the Battle of the Sexes, I was down 3-2 and Bobby broke my serve at 2-all. This was the most critical moment of the entire match for me. I really felt that I had to win the first set in order to get a psychological advantage over Bobby. But I just kept thinking, "One ball at a time," like a meditation. It helped keep me from letting anxiety sap my energy.

I think it's also important not to get too far ahead of ourselves. I often find that if I think too far down the

> I have always said that a trait that differentiates champions from the good players is that champions are big on awareness—they pay attention to every little detail, and they prioritze. In tennis, for example, little things like the direction and strength of the wind, the area surrrounding the court, or the weather, the sun, the blue sky (it's harder to see the ball with a sunny blue sky), the time of day, or the feel of the surface of the court can completely change your game. A champion will notice the details and adapt. In whatever you are doing, when practicing awareness, you will notice more of the minute details and are more likely to take advantage of the opportunities that others might miss.

road, it is more difficult to focus on what needs to happen now, and things start to fall apart. My favorite way to stop from getting ahead of myself is to break down each task into manageable sizes. Doing so keeps the situation from feeling too daunting and keeps me from feeling overwhelmed—remember, one ball at a time.

For example, in 1968 I had a knee operation. At that time, this was major surgery that resulted in a week's hospital stay, a straight cast, and nearly a year of recovery—not like today when you would have outpatient surgery and be in physical therapy the next day. In fact, my doctor told me, "Don't count on ever playing Wimbledon again." Not the kind of news I wanted to hear. But I knew if I started thinking about Wimbledon when I couldn't even bend my leg, the challenge of getting better was going to seem impossible. My leg had been set in a cast that kept it artificially straight and hyper-extended instead of naturally bent (legs are never set straight nowadays). Scar tissue had built up while my leg was held straight, so once the cast came off I had to crack through the scar tissue just to bend my leg. The pain was excruciating. But instead of focusing on bending it all the way, which I knew I could never do right off the bat, my first goal was to bend my leg a quarter of an inch in a hot tub—that was a task I could actually see myself accomplishing. Once that task was done, I gave myself another small, manageable challenge, until I could finally bend my knee all the way. Musicians do something similar. Most musicians do not start off practicing a new piece by just playing it

Know yourself. To thine own self be true. Discover your truth. However you phrase it, self-awareness is the foundation on which all of these lessons in this book are built.

There are a number of facets to self-awareness. One facet is knowing your abilities and your limitations. For instance, God gave me more blessings on the coordination side than on the music side, even though piano was my first love. As much as I adored music, I just was not as adept at it. It only took me a nanosecond to see which one of these loves would make me feel fulfilled.

What's most important is that we recognize our own abilities and learn how our bodies and minds really work. I make a concentrated effort to be realistic about my strengths and pay attention to my body, to listen to it, and sense what it needs. We are incredible creations, and sometimes we just need to trust ourselves. Knowing yourself is knowing your truth.

through all at once; they break it down into sections and perfect each section before moving on to the next.

Second, I have always tried to live in the now. In fact, I didn't even watch the tapes of the Riggs match until about eight years ago (some of the details in this book I have only just discovered myself!). I think it's fine to talk about the past a little bit, but it is really important not to dwell on it—in other words, if we blow an easy shot, then we should try not to beat ourselves up about it or let it affect the next shot. For instance, in the match against Bobby, I took the few minutes of down time while we switched ends to reflect on what winning the match would mean, to me and to the world, instead of thinking about all the stupid little mistakes I felt I had made so far. It helped me regain my focus.

Sometimes bringing all of yourself to a task is actually knowing when to let go. I always care about the task at hand, and try to follow through, but there are times when I find myself hitting a brick wall. These are times when trying softer can work better—in other words, *relax* and breathe. It is the difference between letting it happen and making it happen. When we try too hard we can be too tense; with muscles rigid and anxiety skyrocketing, there will be no flow to what we are doing.

The bottom line is that bringing all of yourself to a task or situation allows you to be centered, ready, and able to respond to anything that comes your way. And once the task is finished, you have a sense of peace, knowing that you did the best that you can do— whether it was moving forward or letting go.

INSTANT REPLAY

Bring All of Yourself to Everything You Do

Bring all of yourself by completely committing yourself to whatever you do. Take things one step at a time, and break your challenges down into manageable goals and objectives so you do not get overwhelmed. Stay in the now by embracing each moment, being aware, noticing the right details, prioritizing, and staying focused. Avoid dwelling on the past, but also avoid looking so far ahead that you can't see the next step in the process. Finally, learn the difference between letting it happen and making it happen. To enjoy life and make the best of it, try to recognize when it's time to try a different approach, and when it's time to just walk in a new direction.

Chapter Four

See It Happen to Make It Happen

It is an old adage, but it's a true one—seeing is believing.

A large part of preparation is setting a specific goal, choosing a strategy to get there, and then visualizing the outcome—seeing it in your mind so clearly that it's like you are living it before it actually happens.

Before the Battle of the Sexes, I pictured myself in a rally, pictured myself running everything down, making the right choices, believing that I could get to every single ball—like a film. I pictured how I would serve it (flat, topspin, or slice, for example) and where to place it. I saw it in my mind and believed that it had happened so that I could expect it to happen on the court.

A lot of people will talk about getting into an opponent's head as part of their strategy. I don't really do that. I prefer to assess my opponent's strengths and weaknesses quickly and then get my own act together. I just stay on my side of the net and respond to what is hit at me. The ball tells me everything; it tells me whether to hit an offensive, defensive, or neutral shot. In the Battle of the Sexes, I was already familiar with Bobby's strategy and style. Instead of trying to figure out what he was thinking, I obtained an understanding of who he was and how he behaved. I had a long oral history from older players socializing at Lakewood Country Club, which was a public park (as a junior, I was not allowed to play without an adult so I'd listen to them talk about Bobby while waiting for an adult who would agree to play with me). These stories taught me all about his hustling—not just his tennis game. I had also read a lot about him, as well as about other players, because I loved the history of tennis almost as much as I loved playing the sport itself. All that experience helped me visualize playing against Bobby.

I have no idea if we can control our dreams, but I do know I was controlling my thoughts about the match, thinking so positively about it during my waking hours that I think it carried over into my sleep as well. I dreamed about tennis in general and about the upcoming match in particular. The dreams were good; I never had a negative one. In my dreams, I got to every ball. I hit winners. I ran Bobby all over the court. I won, over and over. (Can you guess the score in my dreams? Yes, it was 6-0, 6-0, 6-0.)

During the day, when I visualized the match, I would get all my senses involved in it. I saw the Astrodome filled with spectators. I heard the din of the crowd. Then I pictured playing points within that setting. I saw myself hitting the ball, connecting each time, and winning the point out. A technique I often use is visualizing the court from an aerial view; doing this helps give me perspective on the positioning of the players, and where I have space to hit the ball—behind them or to the open area. I actually just found out about a year ago that my brother R.J. did the same thing when he pitched!

Try writing down your goals four times a year. Write down two personal, two business, and two health goals for the next two, five, and ten years. When you set your goals, your brain will enter them into your subconscious. These written goals will give you direction and focus.

I also thought of challenges I could run into—bad line calls, a great serve by Bobby, a screaming audience of thousands, even an electrical blackout—and visualized how I would handle each of them. I realized that I needed to keep the game intimate, especially in this gigantic stadium that was never meant for tennis. I visualized staying focused on what was happening on the court; not looking at the audience or even acknowledging they were there, and not talking to anyone on the sidelines until the match was over. This mental problem-solving gave me comfort because I felt confident that I was prepared to handle anything that might come up.

In a match, you are hitting the ball 25 percent of the time—which means that you are *not* hitting the ball 75 percent of the time. How you use the time when you are not physically actively engaged is vital. In the Battle of the Sexes, the changeovers were two minutes instead of the usual one minute to allow for television commercial breaks; I was not used to being idle for that long during a match, but I used that time to re-evaluate and visualize what I would do next. As I mentioned earlier, these brief visualizations made all the difference to me when I was down near the end of the first set. I saw myself taking control of the match, and then I did it.

Roger Federer, the current Number 1 men's tennis player in the world, gives us a wonderful example of using visualization to achieve goals and success. In his recent biography Federer wrote of an experience he had when he was a teenager at a tennis academy in Switzerland. He and the other players were asked to write down their goals. Every single player wrote that they wanted to be in the top 100 of the ATP Tour (the men's professional tour)—everyone except Roger. Roger wrote that he wanted to be in the top 100 and assigned a date to it. Then he wrote a target date for making the top 10, and another date to become the

I remember in 1989, Martina Navratilova came to Chicago with Craig Kardon, her full-time coach, to work out at the Midtown Tennis Club in preparation for the 1990 season (Martina would always decide near the end of the year if she would play the following year.) Craig brought me in as an extra coach, for the "jolts." The first thing I did was ask her, "If you could have one goal for 1990, what would it be?" She told us that she wanted to win Wimbledon singles in 1990. I asked her if that would be enough. She said it would. Martina was journaling every day to measure her mental, emotional, spiritual, and physical abilities. We asked her to bring the journal to the court every day to write down what she felt was important, which she did (she kept it in her racket cover). For instance, if she was trying to change a stroke, she would write that in her journal then replay it to us and we would help fill in any gaps in her process. I also asked her to write her affirmation of commitment to winning Wimbledon. So, every morning and night for more than six months leading up to Wimbledon, Martina wrote, "I won Wimbledon in 1990," as if it had already happened. She visualized it, seeing it over and over again in her mind, like a memory. And it worked! She did win Wimbledon in 1990. (It was her ninth singles win, which to this day is still a record.) She believed it until it became part of her psyche, and then she made it happen.

Number 1 player in the world. He did not just have a pie-in-the-sky dream. He visualized his future and was pretty darn specific about it!

Visualization works in all areas of life, too. I still use the technique, off and on the court. I have done a lot of speaking over the years. I am very shy, and because of that, I can get very anxious before speaking to an audience—yes, even now—so I visualize speaking engagements before I do them.

Before I give a talk, I ask a lot of questions about the crowd. I want to know who is going to be sitting in front of me—will they be old or young, will they be mostly men or women, what are the different cultures—so that I can visualize them. I then think about how I can reach that audience, to make my speech relevant for them. If I am giving a motivational speech, for example, I might prepare by visualizing how the crowd could react to different deliveries of a call to action. Or I will imagine their responses to different parts of my speech, try to see myself connecting with them. I can never be sure how an audience will react, of course, because I don't know their own personal truth, or their perspective. But I remind myself of what has worked in the past, and I'm confident that if I can see it, I can make it happen. I'm also confident that if one approach does not work, I can just take a moment to reflect and try something different—although it still isn't easy.

Visualization is also good for more than just preparation. Sometimes I will use it to slow myself down when I'm playing. Taking a moment to get a picture in my mind helps calm me, gets me centered. I will

People are often surprised to learn that Pete Sampras never won a national junior singles title. The reason? He was always focused on being the best, number one in men's tennis, not in junior tennis. So while he was competitive in junior matches, he had his eyes on the big prize: to be the number one professional player in the world. Pete didn't worry about the Junior rankings when he was developing his game, making sure he had the weapons—like his famous serve—to be the best player in the world. He played up, competing in matches against players in higher levels and older age groups, to get important experience. He didn't win all of those matches. Winning in the Juniors just was not important to him—developing his game was. All his energy was directed toward his ultimate goal, with none to waste on fretting about the Juniors. Now, *there* is visualization on a big scale!

picture how I want to serve—with topspin, a slice, or flat-and where I want the ball to land—I see the trajectory, and the spot where it is to land (this is a big spot, not the size of a dime), and I will sometimes picture it from an aerial view as well. This gives me a goal. Then I stop my visualization, and move from seeing into the future to being in the now, and I execute.

The bottom line on visualization is that *we are what we think*. If it seems as if the weight of the world is on our shoulders, we are almost certain to perform as if it is. We'll just be weighed down. If we think negatively, think we cannot do something or be something, we will never do it or be it. I am always reminded of Althea Gibson, the first person of color to win a major tennis championship (French Open 1956), who titled her 1958 autobiography *I Always Wanted to Be Somebody*. Her title reveals her secret: she had a vision of "being someone," of making her dreams come true against all odds. She saw it, she believed it, and then she made it happen.

Obviously we can't imagine every challenge that may arise in a situation—as the poet said, "the best laid plans of mice and men often go awry." But that does not mean we have to get derailed because an unexpected situation arises. Just because a problem did not occur to us in the preparation stage, it does not mean it is insurmountable. Once I've visualized and prepared as much as possible, I try to let go and trust myself—I know that I'm okay and that everything I need is inside of me. So I just have to allow my instincts to kick in. And if something comes up that I didn't think of during my preparation, I just stop for a moment and change my perspective to this new situation by taking in the new information and visualizing the solution for this new set of circumstances. I am clear about my goal, I am centered, and I adjust.

Visualization works not only for single tasks, but also for the big picture. Say you want to make a significant change in your life—a new profession, for instance. First visualize what the new place or position looks like—the important details, even colors. Next visualize what it will take to get to that new place—the preparation you will have to do, any training you might need, the roadblocks you might encounter, the issues you may have to face, then focus your visualization on what you will do to prepare and respond to these situations. Finally, visualize the benefits of having that new position. Think positively and believe you have attained your new goal until it becomes a part of your consciousness. This helped me with the Battle of the Sexes, when I visualized all the wonderful things that could happen if I won, imaging even the small ways that my win might affect other people's lives in a cumulative way.

Once you start using visualization, you will soon see getting to that new place in your life or finishing a big task is not as daunting as you thought.

INSTANT REPLAY

See It Happen to Make It Happen

Visualization is a great way to give yourself a call to action, whether it's to accomplish a goal or create change in your life. You never know what is going to happen in a situation until it happens. But you can do research and gather information so you can visualize in detail how you want things to go: envision the situation and your desired outcome, feeling it, using all your senses to experience the scene in your mind until you really believe it. Visualization is about being in the process, focusing on what you can do to be prepared and to respond to a variety of circumstances, and living things out in your head until they become part of your consciousness.

See It Happen

....

Chapter Five

Labeling
and
Assumptions

We often say in our World TeamTennis office: "The first three letters of 'assume'—that is what you become when you assume."

A bit crass? Maybe. But the point is, never assume. Ever.

I have never liked assumptions because I do not like labels. People have labeled me my whole adult life: I have been "the tennis player," "the feminist," "the gay and lesbian and equal rights pioneer." Of course, I am all of these things, but I am not just any one of them. I have never understood why people feel the need to put labels on others. Labeling people minimizes who they really are. It's the easy way out, it narrows the thought process, and can trivialize something that could be seen in a much deeper way. Assumptions and other judgments also separate people into categories, but I believe in uniting people. My whole life has been about getting people to evoke change and to create peace, happiness, and harmony for us all. Labeling works against those kinds of efforts.

My match with Bobby Riggs provides a great example of how making assumptions and labeling can be a mistake. The match was cast as the man vs. the woman, the Battle of the Sexes. A grudge match for the ages. (By the way, I hated the idea of the match being a "battle." I always want men and women to work together, not battle against one another.)

Five minutes before the match started, Jerry Perenchio came up to me and said, "I'm sure you're not going to want to do this, but would you mind being carried out into the Astrodome in this?" He pointed to a gaudy, gold gilt Egyptian litter with feathers coming out of the top of the chair. Because the women's movement was so prevalent in 1973, his opinion may have been limited, and he may have thought I would never even consider such an idea. I knocked his socks off when I agreed. "Are you kidding? Why not!" I said, smiling. "This is great! It's fun, it's entertaining. I'm a performer. Let's not forget, it's show time, baby!"

I knew I couldn't take myself or what I was doing too seriously. Don't get me wrong, it was a serious situation. But that much was obvious, so I had no need to reinforce the fact by keeping a solemn attitude. Anything I could do to lighten my mind was a very good thing. In fact, it calmed me down to get onto that litter and allow myself to be carried to the court like Cleopatra. At that point, all my training and preparation was done. It was time to let go and play. I only had one real problem with the whole scene—I'm afraid of heights! I thought they were going to drop me. (Of course they didn't.) We made a grand entrance and it really set the right mood, bringing a little lightheartedness to a very tense situation for both us players and for the audience. As they say, laugh and others will laugh with you. I find the ability to laugh at myself not only can put me at ease in a situation, it can break the ice and put others at ease as well.

Besides, I love surprising people and throwing stereotypes to the winds. Being well known for something makes it easy for people to form an opinion about you. That is human nature. We are always trying to understand the world around us by defining it in ways that make sense to us. But what I do not like is people assuming that the exterior tells you everything about

For the Battle of the Sexes, I wanted my tennis dress to be just right—I like when form follows function and both work together—and I had selected certain pieces of jewelry that were special to me. Actually, I love paying attention to the details of my appearance when I have to perform. This may not exactly fit in with some people's preconceived notions about female athletes and strong women.

The wonderful fashion designer Ted Tinling, a dear friend, created my tennis outfit for that night—a beautiful mint green sweater and a dress with a blue bodice to match my blue shoes, dotted with small mirrored accents. Ted and I went over every detail several times. He called me "Madame Superstar," and I certainly did not mind. I could always be a little bit of a diva around him, which was fun for me. He was the best.

the interior. It is far simpler to categorize what someone is on the outside—a tennis player, a feminist, a woman—than to narrowly define who they are on the inside, and it is plain wrong to make assumptions about who a person really is based on such superficial labels. We would all be a lot better off as a society if we stopped assuming people are the way we judge them to be based on their exteriors and tried to see things from their perspective. Bobby made the assumption that "girls play a nice game of tennis, for girls"—and we all saw how that assumption panned out!

There are other kinds of assumptions that have always bothered me. I cannot tell you the number of people I see in social situations who assume they are so well known that they do not need to introduce themselves. Almost every time I meet someone new, depending on the situation, I stick out my hand and say, "Hi, I'm Billie Jean." Every single time, even if I'm at a sports event or a meeting where there is a good chance they know me or are expecting me.

I have had the opportunity to meet many successful CEOs of major corporations, each famous in his or her own right, and yet almost every single time these people have introduced themselves to me, never assuming that I already know who they are. You know how it is to fumble around in your mind, trying to come up with a name? Well, if you say your name, the worst thing that happens is the person comes right back with: "Don't be silly, I know who you are." Introducing yourself, even if you think you should be recognized, eases any pressure and sets a positive tone for your encounter. It levels the playing field and creates a more centered environment where everyone feels more at ease.

One final observation going back to the Battle of the Sexes. Bobby was portrayed as a complete male chauvinist pig, right? Well, get this: Our famous male chauvinist actually was taught how to play tennis by a female coach, Eleanor "Teach" Tennant.

Bet you never assumed *that.*

INSTANT REPLAY

Labeling and Assumptions

When you assume, when you label people, you are limiting your ability to see the whole of who they are. This is true when you label yourself, too! Just enjoy who you are and have fun with your life—try laughing instead of judging, acceptance instead of criticism. Trust your instincts, gather facts, listen to your gut, but also try to see things from other people's perspectives; I find it best to remember that everyone has their own individual truth, their own interpretation. The flexibility this kind of openness will give you in dealing with others will serve you in all areas of your life, in business and in personal relationships.

Chapter Six

Pressure Is a Privilege

It was the 1999 Women's Soccer World Cup final at the Rose Bowl in Pasadena, California. With the game scoreless after regulation and overtime, U.S. goalie Briana Scurry made a critical save on a Chinese penalty kick. Moments later, up stepped Brandi Chastain. If she made her penalty kick, the U. S. team would defeat China and win the World Cup.

Brandi stood on the field alone, in front of the Chinese goalie, with more than 90,000 screaming fans cheering her on. She was looking pressure right in the face. Brandi kicked the ball and scored—and in doing so, truly understood what a privilege it was for her to be in that magic moment.

Yes, it was a privilege to have reached a moment that produced such a high level of pressure. Great moments carry great weight—that is what pressure to perform is all about. And though it can be tough to face that kind of pressure, very few people get the chance to experience it.

"Pressure is a privilege" is one of my favorite sayings. It is something I have believed in since I first stepped onto the tennis court as a competitor. I know it may seem odd to call pressure a privilege, but with every success come certain pressures that go with it. Like many people who succeed in challenging fields, I seem to embrace that pressure and thrive on it—as the pressure mounts, I get calmer and more focused.

We all feel pressure from different sources and situations over the course of our lives. Some people don't feel that they are wired to deal well with pressure. And although in certain areas I usually use pressure to motivate me, there are situations off the court where I feel anxious from pressure (like writing this book while staying on top of my other obligations). But part of what helped me transform the way I think about pressure and what has allowed me to embrace it is the realization that negative reactions to intense situations have more to do with fear than with the pressure itself.

As I said, I am shy. Very shy. I remember being in fifth grade and feeling too afraid to get up in front of the class and give an oral book report. I just could not do it. My teacher did not know what to make of the situation, so she called my parents and said, "Billie Jean is going to get an unsatisfactory grade in reading if she doesn't give her oral book report. I don't know what the problem is—doesn't she read?" My father was speechless. I loved to read and my father had seen me read dozens of books. He could not figure out how an "unsatisfactory" was possible for me.

My parents sat me down and asked what the problem was. I told them the truth—I was scared. The thought of getting up and talking in front of the class absolutely terrified me—I thought my heart would beat out of my chest and I would die right there. And it was something I loved—tennis—that would eventually help me get over this hurdle.

Every player knows that if you win a tournament, you have to say a public "thank you" afterward. I realized winning a tournament was the eventual—and desired!—result of all of my hard work, and whether I liked it or not, the pressure of public speaking came with the privilege of winning. And of course I wanted to win tournaments. From the start, my desire to win

Many players have a ritual that they do to stay in the moment or repeat when they feel they are trying too hard or are not playing up to their personal expectations. In my case, I would bounce the ball twice before I would serve; if I was tense or unfocused, I would do it again. I would take long, slow breaths, breathing in for four counts (pushing my stomach out) and breathing out for four counts (pulling my stomach in). This calms me down, relaxes me, and makes me feel secure. I still do this in a variety of situations. I visualize filling my lungs with air, and I literally put my hand on my middle to reconnect me to my body and help me get centered, integrated. I cannot emphasize enough how big I am on using breathing exercises to stay in the process, whether my goal is winning a match or completing another task.

was huge, but my fear of speaking in front of an audience seemed even stronger.

I wanted to win and I wanted to get over my fears. I soon got the chance to test myself: the day came that I won a thirteen-and-under event in Santa Monica and had to stand up and thank everyone. Even though I was scared, I knew I had to do it, so I stood there and, in a soft voice and with my knees knocking, managed to eek out my various thank-yous. When I was done, I realized it wasn't so bad! I certainly didn't die. Not only did winning this tournament help me overcome my fear of public speaking, I also won a radio. Victory has its rewards!

This was my first experience with "pressure is a privilege." I worked long and hard to get to the point where I could win that match, and it was a privilege to receive that award. But it was very clear that the pressure of public speaking came with the privilege of being the winner, and it always would in my world.

Another example: When I was eleven years old and just starting to play tennis, I would sleep with my racket and dream of winning on Wimbledon's Centre Court. Finally, in 1961 at the age of 17, I got the chance. Karen Hantze (Susman) and I, unseeded, had beat the top-seeded doubles team in the quarterfinals and were now facing the third seeded pair of Margaret Smith (Court) (yes, the same woman whom Bobby beat before me) and Jan Lehane (O'Neill) for the ladies' doubles title. I had won my first adult singles title only a year before, in Philadelphia. But this was one of my dreams—a Wimbledon title. I lived for it, wanted it more than anything, and I knew how much of a privilege it was to be there.

Was there pressure? More than you can imagine. On top of all the obvious pressure, my coach was dying of cancer, and he'd often told me of his own dream to coach a player through a Wimbledon win. It was very important to him, and so very important to me. He held on and died the day after Karen and I won 6-3, 6-4. I was so happy to be able to give him that last bit of gratification.

Many times, privilege and pressure just go together— if you want the privilege, you are also asking for the pressure. But sometimes pressure is not a choice or decision. Sometimes you get pushed into it. Getting that nudge is not uncommon, and can be a great way to get over the nerves that pressure can bring. In the case of the Battle of the Sexes, I didn't feel like I had a choice; I played Bobby Riggs because Margaret Court lost, and I felt that if I didn't take him up on his chal-

There is a saying in sports—"Give me the ball!" Champions call for the ball because they want to prove themselves, they want to play their game, and they see having the ball as an opportunity to make something happen—to score, set up someone else, or win for themselves and/or their team. Certainly there is pressure with having the ball, but champions don't run away from this pressure—they recognize that taking the ball (or making a speech, leading a family, or any pressure situation) and being in the spotlight can be scary, but it is also a privilege and an honor—not many people get this chance to shine. Champions grab the ball and go for it, with confidence and adrenalin flowing. You can dread getting the ball or view it as an opportunity, a chance to show them what you've got and to make a difference. After all, if you don't have the ball, you can't score.

lenge the women's movement and our struggles for equality in sports and beyond could have taken a serious blow. I was not looking for that match, it was just an opportunity that arose—one that I initially did not even want.

I did ultimately accept the challenge, but talk about pressure! Along with what was at stake—the advancement of the women's movement and women's sports, not to mention my own pride and reputation—I was going to be watched by millions of people! You would have to be made of stone not to be at least a little nervous at that prospect. And everywhere I turned, there was Bobby talking trash in the media, which had plenty of its own remarks to make. (There were also very few women sports writers working at the time, and none of them were sent to cover the match.)

At first, I felt obligated to play Riggs, but I chose to embrace as a privilege the pressure that threatened to overwhelm me. This changed my entire mindset and allowed me to deal with the situation more calmly. And as time went on I began to see the match as something I *got* to do instead of something I *had* to do.

Sometimes pressure will take you out of your comfort zone, and not many people like that feeling—after all, it is called a "comfort zone" for a reason! You might not believe it, but because pressure is a motivator, and going outside of the zone can be a very good thing. Embracing new opportunities is truly the best way to see how far you can go, and that leads to growth—not to mention fun! And what is life without growth and fun?

Just before the men's PGA Tour's 2003 Colonial tournament in Fort Worth, Texas, Annika Sorenstam and I talked on the phone. Annika was to be the first woman golfer ever to participate in the Colonial, and the first woman to participate in a PGA event since Babe Zaharias in 1945. The tournament was being billed as the twenty-first century version of the Battle of the Sexes, and her presence caused a lot of controversy; even one of the participants, Vijay Singh, was quoted as saying Annika had no business being there and he hoped she would not make the cut.

Needless to say, the pressure on Annika was enormous, and she was calling me to exchange ideas on how to handle the situation. It turns out that she handles pressure the same way I do—by facing her problems head on, and by asking for help when she needs it. It was inspiring to listen to her talk about how she wants to make the crucial putts in a golf tournament and how she cherishes each moment. Her recognition that pressure is a privilege is what makes her a champion—on the golf course and in life.

Annika did a great job and beat nearly a dozen players, but ultimately didn't make the cut. Sometimes winning is simply being given that chance, that opportunity, and taking it.

So, okay, pressure is a privilege. But how do we really handle the pressure? Well, everyone handles pressure differently, but my experiences have taught me a few ways to stay focused and keep from imploding, even out of my comfort zone.

As we have already discussed, the first important step when faced with a stressful situation is to realize that we are fortunate to have this opportunity and the pressure that goes along with it. Nothing great ever comes easy. Great accomplishments often require struggle, focused, intense preparation, and sometimes even setbacks—but we can make it easier by being positive. For example, when I play a match, I can't control what the court will be like, how the weather will be, or what my opponent is going to do. I can only control my approach. Far out from an event, I sometimes get really anxious and fearful. I can be very negative and critical of myself. But I am always working to catch myself when I get this way. I quickly shift my perspective; I choose to be positive.

This allows me to relax, to really focus instead of getting distracted by that anxiety and fear. Try choosing to be positive and appreciate the opportunities you have, regardless of how challenging they may be, and see how it changes things for you.

The next step may not be an issue for some, but could be inconceivable to others: We've got to face our challenges head-on. I take a moment to decide how I want to approach the opportunity, and then I create my vision for the experience (remember our discussion about visualization?). And forgive yourself from the start for any setbacks that may occur because no one is perfect. One of the worst things we can do is stick our head in the sand—the cause of the pressure will not usually go away by ignoring it and in some cases can get even worse. In fact, sticking your head in the sand can actually bring on more pressure, because hiding out allows the problem to blow up to epic proportions in your mind. Things are rarely as bad as we can make them seem in our heads. Shifting our perspective so that we can see challenges as chances to learn, grow, excel, and live up to our potential can give us the confidence to face whatever life brings us.

Once you are able to stand your ground and face the pressure, it's time to slow down and focus. First, be clear about your goals and what is expected of you, then focus on what the real pressure is and think about ways to embrace it. If the pressure of your project is a tight deadline, try enlisting the help of colleagues or delegate some of the work. If the pressure is that the task is a massive undertaking, look at how you can break it down and prioritize the smaller pieces. If the pressure is singing a solo or giving a speech in front of a large audience, practice singing or speaking in front of friends and family until you are comfortable performing for others. Of course, for some people, getting up in front of family and friends may create even more pressure, and other people prefer to practice in front of strangers. Personally, I like to practice with absolutely no one is in the room, but each person has to decide what is the least stressful situation for them.

Asking for help is a simple element in embracing and working with pressure, yet it is not often taken advantage of. I didn't ask for help enough when I was younger because I was all about "just doing it"—sucking it up and not about acknowledging or dealing with my feelings. Now I know better. Having a good mentor, counselor, friend, or therapist can be vital for success. These people can offer feedback and ideas on how to approach things differently, and may have a wealth of experience to share. Building the team you need to deal with whatever pressure you have, to finish your task, or to feel better, is essential. It takes courage to ask, but it is worth it. And you'll find that people often want to help!

I believe in the power of teamwork and the importance of good mentors, so I often seek help from the many talented people in my life. For instance, I went to Frank Brennan, Sr., my longtime coach, and asked him to help me with strategy for the match against Bobby Riggs. And at the match, I had another coach, Dennis Van der Meer, at my side for guidance and support.

Realizing that you cannot do everything alone and asking for help is something that a lot of people find difficult to do. I am still a firm believer in doing things for yourself when you can, but I know it also takes strength to build a team that will help you achieve your goal—and often doing so will connect you to others who want to achieve the same goal. Our group at World TeamTennis is a perfect example—there is absolutely no way I could have executed the forming and running of this effort by myself.

Handling pressure is a process. The more you focus on the privilege, the better you will handle it. Sometimes, even now, when I walk into a room to give a speech to a large crowd, I think about those days of being so shy and winning that first tournament or what I did that night against Bobby Riggs, and I realize how privileged I was to be in those situations. I think, if I can handle those pressures, I can certainly handle this one. Believe me, if the girl who almost flunked because of an oral book report can go on to handle the kind of pressure I face now on a regular basis, you can do it too.

INSTANT REPLAY

Pressure Is a Privilege

The moments of great pressure in your life—speaking in public, interviewing for a big job or the school of your dreams, dealing with health issues, working through difficulties with someone you love, raising a child—are borne out of the importance of the situation. It is a privilege to have such opportunities—to be trusted to lead a meeting, to be a desired job candidate, to love someone or be loved, to be a parent—and so the pressure that comes with them must be seen as a privilege also. If you can see it that way, you can handle almost anything with calm and grace.

Chapter Seven

Champions
Adjust

Life is short. Sometimes you just have to act. This is the time when you rely on a reservoir of memories, actions, and ideas. If you have prepared well enough, they will be there when you need them.

As I walked into the Astrodome for my match with Bobby, I felt ready. The preparation was done, there was no more practicing to do. From this point on it was all about knowing myself, knowing what would work, knowing what would not. My thoughts were simple, fueled by a basic premise: be fit, be focused, be ready.

My normal strategy in matches is to get points over quickly—and since I had never played a match requiring three out of five sets, I needed to pace myself. After talking to my coaches and discussing many different scenarios, I had planned to play an aggressive, serve-and-volley game against Bobby. Then, something happened that proved to me the value of being on your toes, being ready for anything, and trusting your instincts. As I walked from the baseline to the umpire's chair a few minutes before the match started, I considered that Bobby and I were 26 years apart in age, and that while I knew I was in great shape, I did not know what kind of shape he was in. So I changed my strategy on the spot. I decided not to end points quickly, but do just the opposite—I would get him into long rallies, back and forth, early in the match, still going to the net when it made sense, but running him as much as possible. It did not matter if I won the point or not; I would just wear him out. This plan would give me a better chance to win. I visualized that for just a second or two, no more, then said to myself, "That's it. Do it."

There I was, totally ready and centered, having spent months practicing and preparing a sharp, explosive game, and in the space of two minutes I had changed my entire approach—making perhaps the most important strategic change a tennis player can make—seconds before the match began. If after five or six long points Bobby wasn't tired, I would have to re-assess the situation. I evaluated the situation and trusted my instincts. And it worked beautifully. He did get tired.

After the match started, I relied on my instincts for yet another change in plans that ultimately paid off. I noticed that Bobby was getting more tired when he was serving. I took a few steps forward so that I was standing very close to the service box to return the serve. My mindset was simple. I wanted to put the pressure back on Bobby and leave him with less time to prepare his next shot. Then I could run him back and forth, but from a position of strength. I would be in charge. I knew that, no matter how hard or soft he served or how much spin he put on the ball, I could handle it even in this closer position. But this strategy was not permanent—I could always move back for the next serve if I needed to.

These moments taught me an important lesson that I have taken throughout the rest of my life: to prepare fully, and then, based on that preparation, to totally trust my own instincts, be ready for anything, and be nimble. As my parents always said, there are no guarantees in life. But champions march right up and seize opportunities and are prepared to make unexpected changes to the plan.

Often in life you find yourself facing decisions.

Sometimes they are big, sometimes they are small. I try to always rely on a combination of my instincts and facts to make the decision. In other words, collect the facts and then go with your gut. And because I have faith in my instincts and confidence in my training skills, I can test the waters with a new strategy, knowing I am prepared enough and nimble enough to adjust again, should I need to. And the good news was that, in my match against Bobby, my instincts were right and the adjustment worked out beautifully.

INSTANT REPLAY

Champions Adjust

If you take the time to prepare yourself thoroughly for the challenges in front of you, you will have a foundation of resources to draw upon in a critical moment. Pause and center yourself, gain your focus, and visualize your desired outcome. Trust your instincts and your foundation, observe every detail, and adjust your approach as necessary.

Chapter Eight

Never Underestimate Your Opponent

Of all the statements Bobby Riggs made about our match, the one that resonates the loudest with me to this day is what he said after jumping over the net to shake my hand:

"I really underestimated you."

You've got to hand it to Bobby; he didn't have to say those words to me. He could have come up with all kinds of excuses for losing in straight sets. In one of the last interviews of his life, for the Tennis Channel, Bobby elaborated on his statement:

> I was so confident, I made the classic mistake that any-
> one can make when they think they're so good and they

underestimate their opponent...If you underrate your opponent and overrate yourself you're in trouble right away. I beat Margaret Court 6-2, 6-1, I figured Margaret was a better player, so what chance was Billie going to have? I gave her everything—I said, "You want to play 3 out of 5 sets? Fine, we'll play best 3 of 5. You want to use Wilson balls? We'll use Wilson balls." I figured, why not? She's got two chances—slim and none, and slim just left town. That was my attitude going into it.

Bobby told the truth, and in doing that, he shined a light on an issue that is very important to me. It's always a mistake, in any job or task, to believe a challenge is not great enough to give it your full focus and effort.

Bobby was nothing if not confident, and of course, confidence is key when dealing in any situation. But just assuming we are better than other people is dangerous—remember what we said about assumptions! It's easy to get lulled into a false sense of security by relying on first impressions or hearsay, and if we don't dig deeper to find out our competitors' strengths and weaknesses and how to combat them, we are not bringing all of ourselves to what we are doing.

I'm a firm believer in using history to help prepare. The more we know about our opponents and our situations, the better prepared we will be. Bobby and I were both from Southern California, so growing up I had always heard stories about him and his great career. He had won Wimbledon's triple crown (singles, doubles and mixed doubles) in 1939 and was a former Number 1 player in the world. I studied and understood his game. He was a tough competitor, and I respected him.

When we played in 1973, Bobby finally got the match he wanted, though not the outcome he expected. As he said afterward, he underestimated me. But I never underestimated him. I figured, even though he was doing all those interviews, he also was practicing and playing sets like crazy.

However, it seems that was not the case. In a Tennis Channel interview Larry Riggs spoke about how he tried to get his father to focus. "I said, 'Dad, we need to practice,'" Larry commented. "But it was always, 'I need to do this interview,' or 'I need to do that TV show.' I kept telling him, 'Dad, you're going to get killed.' He kept saying, 'I know what I'm doing.'"

I always think it is far better to overestimate your opponent than to underestimate him or her. The fact that I overestimated how much preparation Bobby was

There is a saying in sports—don't leave it in the gym. It means that you can sometimes overdo things when you are preparing by making yourself over-tired or too tense; you do not want to play the match before you even get out there. As with all things, balance is important to preparation. The key is to really know yourself, your needs, and your limits. You want to train well and wisely, and bring your best to the match itself.

doing did not hurt me. I ended up completely prepared for anything.

Being appropriately confident and being appropriately prepared are two lessons that were instilled in R.J. and me by my mother and father at the earliest age. We were also taught that preparing and bringing your "A" game to everything—bringing all of yourself—is a way of showing respect for your opponent and yourself, another important character trait from my parents. Expecting the best from your opponents and preparing for it shows that you have high esteem for their abilities.

"I made a mistake," Bobby admitted in the Tennis

Channel interview. "When you underestimate your opponent, you're in trouble right away. She played a great match. Her tactics were good. Mine were wrong. I underestimated her."

INSTANT REPLAY

Never Underestimate Your Opponent

You will show respect for yourself and for your opponent's abilities, and for whatever challenge is before you by bringing all of yourself to the situation. If you do this, you will not often be caught by surprise, you will be focused, calm, and centered, and you will be able to perform at the top of your game. But be wary of over-preparing to the point where you have worn yourself out before the critical moment has even arrived. Find the balance. Don't leave it in the gym.

Chapter Nine

Perspective Is Priceless

Obviously tennis is, in many ways, the dominant force in my life. If I had not become a tennis player, it is likely you never would have heard of me. But I have made sure that tennis is not the only force in my life.

Growing up, I was blessed to have parents who gave me their unconditional support. My dad was often working two jobs and my mother sold Tupperware and Avon in order to be able to afford my and my brother's activities. They spent countless hours driving us to—or figuring out how to get us to and from—practices, games, and tournaments. (I remember my mother taking me to my first 15-and-under national tournament in Middletown, Ohio. We could only afford to take the train, and because I was a minor, my poor mother who suffers from horrible motion sickness had to chaperone me. The trip was three and a half days, each way, in coach, sleeping in our seats. I don't know how my mother survived it.) My mother attended many of my matches when I was young, and my father would join her every chance he could. Seeing both of them in the stands together was rare. They tried just as hard to get to R.J.'s games, even though our games were often at the same time. I look back on it now and am still amazed at how much they sacrificed for my brother and me.

But although my parents were supportive, they were not involved in the intricate details of my athletic career. They were my first "financial backers," which was tough with both R.J. and me playing high level sports at the same time. I remember weekends that I did not compete because my family could not spare the $2 tournament entry fee. But soon after I started playing, the Long Beach Tennis Patrons organized themselves and started supporting Long Beach's four best young players—two girls and two boys (Susan Williams and I were the girls; Jerry Cromwell and Alan Robbins were the boys). Jerry Cromwell was one of my closest, dearest friends, and was the Number 1 junior player in Long Beach. Susan's, Jerry's, and my parents organized the carpooling and such so that everyone shared the responsibilities. That support took a lot of pressure off my family.

Also, my mom was not as into sports and was never totally engrossed in the matches she attended; she checked the score sporadically but she actually spent most of the time visiting with the other parents. She loved to socialize almost as much as watching me play. With the carpooling and seeing the same people at events, we had all become a kind of extended family. I don't mean to make it seem as if she didn't care what happened—she was there to support me and wanted me to be happy, and besides, I loved that she was not all over me the way some parents were with their children. She knew what I did on the tennis court was not do or die. She knew there was more to life than tennis.

When my parents couldn't be in the stands, they would always ask me the same questions when I got home. My mother would ask, "Are you really liking this? Did you have fun?" My father, the jock, often asked, "Are you practicing enough—or too much? Did you learn anything?" "Did you try your best?" They didn't ask me if I won or what the score was. All they cared about was my happiness and whether or not I had done my best. Talk about having good perspective.

But still, I got serious about tennis, and fast. When we're young it is impossible to have perspective, and I was no different. I became absolutely obsessed with tennis—I slept in my tennis sweater and with my racquet, practiced constantly, read every tennis book I could get my hands on, and played in every match I could. My father felt I was getting a little too serious. Once, when I was still very young, I displayed a bit of a temper on the court. After the match my father told me if he ever saw me lose my temper again he was going to take my racket away. Then, just to make sure he got his point across, he took my racket to the garage and turned on the power saw. I thought he was going to saw my racket in half! Of course he didn't. He was just trying to make a point, and he succeeded—for the moment. (I would still occasionally lose my temper on the court, but I continued to work on maintaining good perspective.)

About that same time, another experience gave me a sense of perspective about how to handle trouble on the court. I had lost early in a tournament, 6-0, 6-0 and the Long Beach *Press-Telegram* put the story on the front page of the sports section. I had won all kinds of matches but never had made the front page, and now, there it was—one of my most crushing defeats. When I saw the piece I was embarrassed, humiliated, and devastated.

"I'm never going to allow you to read your press clippings again," my father said, "because all they're talking about is yesterday. You need to focus on today and tomorrow." Truer words were never spoken. To this day, I rarely read press clippings, thanks to that lesson.

While my father was teaching me to have perspective in my sport, my mother was teaching me to have perspective in my life. Even when I started getting really good at tennis, my mother had me keep up my piano lessons and church activities. I liked doing these things, so it wasn't as though she forced me—but even if I didn't want to do them, there wasn't really a choice! Mom's decisions were a done deal; she did not waver. And of course I still had chores to do around the house. Expanding my experiences off the court certainly made me well rounded, and left the impression that there was more to life than tennis.

This gift of perspective is one of the most valuable of many lasting gifts my parents gave me. It is also what got me through the match with Bobby Riggs. I am not saying I did not feel any pressure about playing Bobby, because I did. And I have already shared with you some of the ways that I dealt with that pressure. But keeping perspective is what ultimately helped me through it.

Throughout the several crazy weeks leading to the match, I tried not to get too caught up with Bobby's histrionics. He was spouting his male-chauvinistic propaganda to anyone who would listen—in television interviews, newspapers, magazines, you name it—and criticizing me and my gender to millions of Americans. People got angry at Bobby for his lip, and everyone started picking sides, which brought the hype about the match to a fever pitch. But no matter what he said, I never took anything personally and he never managed to offend me. I just laughed it off. In fact, I enjoyed him. He was really very funny, and he was promoting the match, fueling my fire to stay disciplined.

I also sensed an advantage in all that blabbing. I wanted him to keep talking, keep expending energy, and keep digging a nice little hole for himself. I wanted the hype to be about him, for him to take the pressure, to take the spotlight. I needed to keep my focus on the match—the important thing was for me to win, in order to help the causes for which I was fighting so hard—and not get involved in the three-ring circus Bobby was creating.

Throughout my career, I struggled to keep a similar

sense of perspective whenever I lost a match. Losing was always very painful for me—I would spend a couple of days after a loss being self-critical. My mother always said that it was okay to have these once in a while, but that you had to bounce back quickly and move on. I have tried to follow her advice. And I've learned a lot. Eventually, after a disappointment, I could see these times not as losses, but as chances to evaluate what went wrong and figure out my strengths and weaknesses so that I could be that much better the next time.

For me, perspective is an ongoing process of growth. Does losing hurt? Absolutely. Not getting what you have worked so hard for and wanted so desperately can hurt, and there is no way around that. Real life is painful at times and difficult. If you embrace that fact, it makes life much less stressful. But you cannot wallow in it. Instead, try stepping back for a minute and looking at the big picture. First ask yourself, how important is it, really, that you did not win in this situation? Is it just pride talking, or does your performance have a larger effect? If it is that important and you have a chance to go for it again, then do it. But if it is just a matter of your pride taking a hit, or if the situation was just a one-shot deal, then let go and see what you can take away from the experience. Every stage of the journey—preparing, playing, winning, and losing—can also be a time to learn. Evaluate what went wrong and what you did well. See what changes can be made so that when the next opportunity arises, you can use what you learned to create a better outcome. Consider your losses opportunities for feedback, not failures. The added bonus of figuring out how to use that loss is that it will also help you get over the hurt or embarrassment of losing in the first place.

Perspective is all about the words you use to define yourself and your experiences. As a society, we tend to use negative words and to hold tightly to the negative meaning of those words. But if we can define our experiences and outcomes with positive words, if we can change our perspective to a positive one, we will begin to see the growth within ourselves, and may even come to enjoy the process.

Some might say that it is easy to have perspective when your self-esteem is high. But what about people who find it more difficult to find confidence? Maybe you were raised in a family that always said you were nothing, that you were destined to fail. But that's someone else's soundtrack, not yours. It is time to start changing the tapes. Work on replacing those negative internal conversations with positive ones.

Some coaches teach by breaking their players down, but when I coach young players, I teach by reinforcement: 90 percent positive, 10 percent negative. And that is what I think people need. Humiliation is not a good teaching tool, in my opinion. I prefer to lead by love and not by fear.

Now, this may sound strange, but we can also step back, use perspective, and evaluate a situation when we win. Stopping only to evaluate losses will start a downward slide of only focusing on the negative. Just as it is important to know our weaknesses, we have to know our strengths. Looking at what we did right will reinforce those good actions so that we can keep repeating them, creating more "winning" situations in our lives.

If perspective has a first cousin, it must be a sense of humor. Part of my parents' lessons about perspective included the advice that I should not take myself too seriously, ever. Tiger Woods and many others have said, "If you can't laugh at yourself, who can you laugh at?" I know I was laughing when they carried me onto the court on that big gold litter. It's important to be able to step back from a serious situation and find the humor in it. Laughter truly is a wonderful answer to many of life's problems. It may sound hokey, but laughter has always worked for me. When I was captain of the U.S.

Fed Cup team (international team competition for women), the players would throw my sayings back at me if I lost my temper for a moment, saying "Billie, pressure is a privilege!" That always made me laugh. Whenever things get too serious, a smile and a little laughter will break the tension and help me regain my perspective, my focus. I rely on my sense of humor almost as much as my backhand.

Finally, to gain proper perspective, try to put everything in context. Whenever I lost an important match, I would get out of the doldrums by saying to myself, "I am doing what I love and getting paid to do it!" Whether it's work, a relationship, schooling, family, or even your role in life, it's common at times to get down in the dumps about some aspect of it. But if you really love your work, your spouse, your partner, your family, or whatever you are doing, remember the big picture. It's not about winning or losing, it is about having the opportunity to be in it, to really *live* your life, to have purpose, and to enjoy it. Being positive and choosing to see all of our experiences as part of a growth process will impact others as well as improving our own quality of life.

And that kind of perspective will keep you going.

INSTANT REPLAY

Perspective Is Priceless

It is a privilege to have this life. And there is more to life than tennis for me, just as there is more to your life than your work. Take a positive view, and eliminate negative words and perspectives. Learn to step back and evaluate both your wins and losses, and enjoy the process of growth. Try to focus on living at your best and meeting your potential—and always keep looking for new opportunities. This will leave you with a sense of fulfillment—the win that matters most.

Pressure Is a Privilege

....

Chapter Ten

Start with Integrity

I find myself always coming back to one major principal that has guided my life: integrity. Everything starts with integrity, which means living with honesty and simply trying to be true to my values. To me, it is the absolute core of a person's character. And although staying true to my values is not always easy, especially if my position is an unpopular one, knowing that I am doing the right thing can make it easier.

Integrity was ingrained in my brother and me every day of our lives by our parents. They were consistent with their honesty, they stood by what they believed in, and they could make the hard decisions. They always tried to do the right thing. As a blue-collar family, we never had a lot of excess money, but my parents always figured out how to support the family. Sometimes my mom took extra part-time work like selling Avon or Tupperware, sometimes my dad moonlighted in a plastics factory. They never crumbled, no matter how tired or stressed out they were, no matter what demands were placed on them. They were a living example of how to have integrity through the worst of times. I love the word "integrity" because it has "grit" right in the middle of it. My parents definitely had grit, because they had unyielding courage in the face of hardship.

The true test of integrity often comes during times of adversity. Our character is revealed in how we handle ourselves in the face of a challenge or setback.

Sometimes it may feel like integrity is a burden— but I think the truth is that every aspect of your life gets better when you can be truly honest with yourself and others. Keeping your integrity and your values intact can benefit you in unimaginable ways. For most of my adult life, I have been known for taking positions that are less than popular for the times. The pressure of speaking up for my values and standing my ground reached critical mass during the Battle of the Sexes match. There was no way I could back down from something I believed was so important to the future of millions of people. I sensed what a big deal it was, and even if I was mistaken, I committed to play it and I knew I had to follow through and deliver. In the end, I may have beaten Bobby and won the prize money, but that was not the ultimate reward of the match—it was getting the validation for women and daughters, implementing social change, getting all people to start thinking differently and work together for equality, and helping others to be the best they could be.

There are also times when integrity is about fighting for what you believe in. Between 1968 and 1970, women tennis players were squeezed out of many tournaments and when we did compete alongside the men at tournaments, they received an average of 11 times the money that we did. We repeatedly asked the men (who were planning to form a men's only players' association) to join forces, but they always said no; we then went to the U.S. Lawn Tennis Association (USLTA) about forming a women's tour and they also refused. At that point we knew that if we were going to ever be treated as equals, we were going to have to do it by— and for—ourselves.

We found our advocate in Gladys Heldman, publisher of *World Tennis* magazine. Gladys brokered a deal

When I was in college at Cal State in Los Angeles, I had to work two jobs to have a little money while also playing tennis. But down the road at UCLA and USC, the men tennis players were getting scholarships.

Athletic scholarships for women did not exist before 1972. If it were not for the tireless efforts of so many supporters, especially the efforts of Congresswoman Edith Green (D-Oregon), Congresswoman Patsy Mink (D-Hawaii) and Senator Birch Bayh (D-Indiana), who stood by what they believed was right, even though it was tremendously unpopular, Title IX would probably still be just a dream. So much of Congress did not want Title IX to ever become a reality, and the bill had failed on the floor many times before passing in 1972. But the legislators knew how absolutely imperative it was to have equal rights in education for all boys and girls, and so they persisted in trying to institute change. Passing Title IX was the correct action in 1972 and it is worth fighting for today. Edith Green, Patsy Mink, and Birch Bayh knew that and it drove them to do the right thing.

with Joseph Cullman III, then President of Philip Morris USA, to sponsor a women's tournament. And in Houston on Sept 23, 1970, Peaches Barkowicz, Rosie Casals, Judy Tegart Dalton, Julie Heldman, Kristy Pigeon, Kerry Melville Reid, Nancy Richey, Valerie Zigenfuss and I (forever known as the "Original Nine") crossed the line in the sand and took a chance. The birth of women's professional tennis as we know it today occurred when the Original Nine signed a symbolic $1 contract with Gladys for the Virginia Slims of Houston, the tournament that would forever change tennis and open the doors for generations of women professional tennis players to make a living playing the sport they love. That tournament led to the formation of the Virginia Slims Series which, by the time I played Bobby in 1973 (the year I also helped form the Women's Tennis Association), had grown to 22 tournaments, offering $775,000 in prize money.

Once we had proven ourselves with a successful tour, the USLTA acted very quickly—and with integrity. In 1973, they broke new ground by paying the women the same as the men, well before that was the popular thing to do. I was thrilled at the way Billy Talbert (U.S. Open tour director), Warren Elcock (president of the USLTA), and the USLTA board handled the situation, and was proud that the U.S. championship was the first to take this important step towards equality.

But having integrity is not just about fighting for what you believe in. It is also about approaching everything in life with honesty and being consistent; sometimes people may feel tempted to let their principles fall by the wayside because they think doing so will make the road smoother, but this couldn't be farther from the truth. It can actually make things harder, not easier. For example, the burden of carrying lies or ill will for long periods of time can weigh us down and drain us emotionally. This drain affects parts of our lives, negatively impacting our relationships, how we relate to our surroundings, and the people around us.

One thing I have always tried to do with regard to being honest and consistent is to keep my promises. I am always striving to meet this goal, and there are times I just do not make it, but I keep trying to be better. The best of both worlds is when our words and actions match. To me, saying one thing and doing another shows a lack of respect for yourself and others, and can destroy the trust that others have in you. I wish we had a culture that looked down on efforts to "get away" with things rather than rewarding them.

I also try to keep listening, to keep an open mind. As

I said earlier, everyone has their own truth, and it is a mistake to assume that our perspective is the only correct one. We are not infallible. We never know when what we believe will turn out to be wrong. I try to allow room for the times when someone will convince me that what she or he believes is right so that I can change my mind. Remember, champions adjust.

But when I really believe, deep down, that something is right, I stand my ground. It can be hard to stand our ground, especially when we feel like we're the only ones speaking out for what we think right. That is why it's so important to surround ourselves with good role models—"A" players who have good values, are emotionally healthy, have a strong moral ground, and who can have a positive influence on our lives. My parents, my partner Ilana Kloss, my friends Holly Hunter, and Elton John, Dennis Alter (CEO of Advanta), who teaches me something every time I see him, and Ed Woolard, my mentor and former CEO of DuPont—these are just some of the people I know I can trust and look to as examples of people who function from a place of integrity.

On the flip side of the coin, I try not to associate with people who are counterproductive, engage in destructive practices, are only outwardly successful, or who are otherwise bad influences.

The higher we rise in sports, in the workplace, and in life, the greater the responsibility to live with integrity. Our actions become more visible and touch more lives as we advance, giving us the opportunity to bring about more good in the world and an equal opportunity to bring about more pain depending on the examples

---

We do not live our lives in a vacuum. It is important to try to respect other people's positions, even if you disagree with them. Remember that their truth or perspective may not be the same as yours, and people sometimes make mistakes or are wrong—we all make mistakes. At times, acting with integrity sometimes means practicing forgiveness, and learning how to ask for it. Tennis is a great metaphor for life: in tennis, people immediately see the consequences of every decision they make with every ball, every shot, learn from what they did right or wrong, adjust their game, keep going, and try to win until the match is over. So if you lie or mess up in some way, try to come clean and make things right again. But don't give up—always keep going, and keep trying to make better choices.

---

we set. Abandoning principles just to move up the ladder can leave us hollow, which then sets us up to fall off that ladder. If someone cheats to win a match, what did he or she really win? If people are deceitful, dishonest, or do not play by the rules, covenants, parameters, or principles agreed to, it not only blows their reputation but can also damage the lives of others.

Many of the problems we are seeing nowadays concerning a lack of integrity stem from the fact that people are putting the emphasis on "outer success"—how much we make, how much we own, how we look, etc.—and not on the "inner success" which brings fulfillment and real happiness. In Western culture we use money as a unit of measurement, and that it's important to recognize and work with that information in order to get just compensation. But the foundation of the equal pay effort is the principle of self-worth. Inner success is what matters; focusing on the inner parts of ourselves is what will ultimately bring us success in those "outer" aspects of our lives, too.

We are bombarded daily with stories of people who have pitched their integrity out the window—politicians who are dishonest, sports figures who are doping, corporate heads who are robbing their companies blind, entertainment celebrities who headline the tabloids—the list is endless. I think sometimes we hear so much about the bad things that are going on that we forget about the millions of people acting with integrity every day in ways both big and small. Let's focus on those people who are doing good things and use them as role models rather than look only to the cautionary tales of superstars who do the wrong thing. Remember, it takes years to build a reputation and you can lose it overnight.

I encourage everyone to look beyond the obvious and find people in their daily lives who set a positive example. Try not to just surround yourself with "yes" people telling you what you want to hear; pick people who are honest and act with integrity. The best role models have conviction in their beliefs, even when being attacked or doubted, and are kind, generous, and have a sense of humor. Some people might find it strange for me to say, but Bobby Riggs is really a good role model. He acted like a true gentleman when the match was done, he behaved with integrity, and he was a great sport. Not to mention, he always had fun, was optimistic, and always kept his word.

I want to get back to the idea of integrity sometimes being a struggle. There have been many times in my life where I have been attacked for what I believe in, or for who I am. For example, when I was knee deep in the effort to get the men and women tennis players to join forces, a friend told me, "No one will pay a dime to watch you birds play." That was very hurtful, and it would have been easy to agree with him. Certainly, many other people did. But deep inside, I knew that was not the truth, and it also wasn't the point, because we were already getting paid—even if it was just a little. Similarly, when we started the Virginia Slims Series, people in the media tried to put a negative spin on it, calling us a bunch of "women's libbers" as if that were something bad. But we knew that we were making an important statement about equality, not just for women athletes, but for all people, everywhere. Dealing with those critics taught me an important lesson: when people attack or criticize you mercilessly, it is usually about *them*, not you. Never take it personally.

Not taking attacks personally is easier said than done. But if we let the critics get to us, the stress can generate negativity that will spill over into other areas of our lives. That negativity has to go someplace, and inevitably can get taken out on everyone around us. In therapy they call it "anger coming out sideways." I remember one specific time when this happened to me—it was in the middle of a match. Now, usually I am completely focused during a match, but all of a sudden I found myself flying off the handle at the umpire, the linesman, my opponent, the crowd—everyone. At the time my off-the-court life was a complete mess; my marriage was a disaster, and I was struggling with my sexuality. Not only were my parents homophobic, but I was too, which made me even more confused. I couldn't talk to anyone about it because I was told the WTA Tour would not happen if I spoke publicly about being a lesbian, which sent me even deeper into the closet. I never like to lie or be deceitful or dishonest. Living in the public eye is stressful enough, but being forced to live a life that went against my own value system of always telling the truth and being honest made it even more difficult. I was basically paralyzed. The anger, shame, and frustration were overwhelming, and I let it affect my demeanor on the court. If I got a bad call I would scream at the linesman; if someone in the audience shouted something at me I would yell back. At the time, I had no mechanism for coping with the criticism, and I did not learn how to handle it until I got into therapy. Thank God for terrific therapists!

When it comes to issues of integrity, it is most important that you can be at peace with yourself when your head hits the pillow every night. For me, that means living true to my principles and being responsible for my own actions. Do not worry about what everyone else thinks; focus on what *you* believe to be good and right. As my mother (and Shakespeare) always says, "To thine own self be true."

INSTANT REPLAY

Everything Starts with Integrity

Living with your integrity and staying true to your values—especially when it's tough to do so—is probably the most important thing you can do to maintain peace of mind and be comfortable in your own skin. It is also a critical element in true success—if you are successful, then you are living according to your value system. Know what your values are—which principles and ethics are most important to you. Surround yourself with people of integrity and let your successes form a wide path for others to follow and share.

Start with Integrity

Chapter Eleven

Aging Is
an Art

There is no getting around getting older, we all know that. But we can actually use my dear friend and foil Bobby Riggs as a metaphor for aging is an art and growing old gracefully. You are probably thinking I have lost my mind saying "graceful" and "Bobby Riggs" in the same breath, but it is true.

Yes, some people thought that parading around with a gaggle of bathing beauties at his age and setting up matches with people decades younger than he was something other than graceful. (He even challenged my executive assistant and close friend, Diane Donnelly Stone, at her tennis club when she was only eleven years old. She lost in a pro set—first to eight winning by two games—8-6. Riggs was fifty-eight by then.) But I look past all that. Bobby never stopped working, playing, having fun, hustling, and re-inventing himself. He continued to find new challenges and keep his life enriched, transitioning from tennis pro to tennis mentor to tennis entrepreneur and business owner. Nothing slowed him down—not age, not adversity, not even prostate cancer, until it eventually took him from us at the age of 77 in 1995.

Over the years I have followed Bobby's lead. After I retired from professional tennis at the age of 40, I transitioned into my life as an entrepreneur, co-founder of World TeamTennis, speaker and businesswoman. His example of remaining vibrant throughout the years has been a powerful one for me. I love where I am now at this point in my life, especially emotionally. I feel free.

My greatest "shero" (my term for a female hero) is my mother. She and my father danced all of their adult lives. They loved to dance the Balboa, something they had been doing since the 1940s, and it kept them in great shape. When my father died in 2006, my mother could have easily sat down in a chair and never gotten up again, but she knew she couldn't stop and do nothing—she had to keep going. Although she lost her dance partner, she still goes dancing every chance she gets and, at eighty-six years old, works out two to three times a week doing weight resistance and cardiovascular training. Recently, about three months before her 86th birthday, she called me all excited and said, "Billie, I walked a mile in twenty-five minutes on the treadmill!" It was priceless—my mother sounded like a giddy ten-year-old!

Many people see aging as a sad inevitability instead of the natural evolution of life, it is such a good message: stay active! It is the absolute best way to grow old gracefully. It is so easy to be sedentary, especially in this day and age with technology putting everything at our fingertips. But once you stop moving, it makes it even harder to get back in the game of life. Exercise is vital to our overall well-being and actually can help you with those achy knees and sore back. It doesn't matter what kind of activity—walking, yoga, stretching, racquet sports, Pilates, swimming, even a stationary bike—what matters is that we get moving.

In case you think becoming sedentary is not an issue for athletes, think again. It happened to me in a big way. For ten years, in my forties, I hardly did any kind of exercise. At around 5 feet 5 inches, I was nearly 200 lbs. And it wasn't because I retired—though I have to admit, not training every day freed up a whole lot of time, and it was nice not to have to live in ice packs every day. I basically stopped working out and started binge eating because I was sad and frustrated by my struggle to get my family to accept my sexuality. I gained a ton of weight. Eating had been a problem for me since childhood, but the goal of winning gave me a reason to stay healthy and playing filled my time, which kept me from having to deal with my emotions. In my transition, my eating and food issues lacked that powerful focus. Binge eating allowed me to push down my emotions, and becoming overweight helped to protect me from people—it was a way to say, "Please leave me alone, I need time."

Finally, at the age of 51, I realized there was no way I was going to get out of this funk without help. As I had learned to do in professional sports, I assembled my support team. I went to my friends Dr. Kay Loveland and Dr. Julie Anthony, both clinical psychologists, who led me to The Renfrew Center for eating disorders. For six weeks I wrestled with the emotional issues that drove my eating—it was painful and a lot of hard work, but it saved my life. I also got back into exercise. And I never stopped again. Even today at age 64 I play tennis two to three times a week and do cardio, stretching, and weight resistance at the gym.

So exercise and mental health are important, but the other important element to the art of aging—or staying young, as I prefer to think of it—is to keep evolving, keep growing (not around the waist, but in your mind and in your activities and interests), and keep looking for new challenges. If you have always wanted to go back to school, open a dress shop, do volunteer work, or learn a new language, instrument, or sport, I encourage you to do it. If you have wanted to take a year off and travel the world like a college student, go ahead—it doesn't matter if you are 25 or 86. If there is one lesson to learn from the baby boomer generation it is that age is just a number and old is not old anymore. For those of us who are still working in our later years or who are taking care of loved ones, try to see the positive side and focus on whatever gives your life meaning. Find whatever time you can to do the things you love and which make you happy—spending time with friends and family, or even doing crossword puzzles—and take every opportunity to learn something new.

Above all, never forget: age does not define you. I learned that in 1973 from the man on the other side of the net. In my wonderful conversations with my mother, I am reminded of it every day. And although I may not be the Number 1 tennis player in the world right now, I would rather be this age than any other.

INSTANT REPLAY

Aging Is an Art

The keys to staying young aren't only found in the cosmetics department or on the surgery table. The best thing you can do for yourself is stay physically and mentally active, keep challenging yourself, never stop learning and growing, and have fun. To maintain proper balance (and everyone has a different definition of what proper balance is for them), relaxation is also necessary. Know your body and know yourself so that you can gauge what you need and want. Above all, enjoy your life!

Chapter Twelve

Leave a Legacy

The women's final of the 2008 Australian Open was a few hours away when I picked up my cell phone at my home in New York City and sent a text message halfway around the world.

"Champions adjust," I typed, "and pressure is a privilege." Then I pressed the send button.

Maria Sharapova's cell phone was not yet turned on in Melbourne, Australia, when I sent her that message. But when she awoke on the morning of the match and turned it on, she saw it. She went on to defeat Ana Ivanovic, 7-5, 6-3, that day, to win her third Grand Slam title in her still relatively short career.

When she left the court, Maria had another text message waiting for her from me. It was simple: "Congratulations! You did great."

Maria mentioned the first text message in her post-match interview. "I had Billie Jean's great words in my mind during the match," she said.

I smiled when I heard her say that. I've known Maria since she was just thirteen—we have a long history together. It has always been a pleasure for me to encourage young people and I have enjoyed watching Maria become one of the great stars of our sport. She is one of many tennis players whom I support. She is smart, classy, appreciates history, and understands her role in shaping the future of tennis.

I am a huge believer in praising and supporting people. The support I received from so many men and women that important night in Houston—from Rosie Casals who was in the television booth to George Foreman, who became my impromptu body guard—still rings in my ears. I never have forgotten their kindness and generosity.

Of the many things I hope I will be remembered for—my legacy—I pray that one of them will be my commitment to mentoring others.

Mentoring is wonderful, and it is very important to

me. I send dozens of text messages to tennis players I know—especially to the captains and players of the Fed Cup (for women) and the Davis Cup (for men), and to others outside the sports world—encouraging them and wishing them well. Over the years, I have encouraged other tennis pros to talk to the younger players, to ask if they can do anything to help them. I am also involved in Pro U, a program run by the Sony Ericsson WTA Tour, which is the tour's umbrella organization for the education of its players. Overseen by Kathleen Stroia, Pro U works with tennis players at the onset of their careers and addresses three core developmental domains: self development, professional tennis development, and business development. A large part of the program is the pairing up of today's young athletes with players from previous generations. As older players (or even retired stars), we are hosts, in a way, and it is our job to be welcoming to this younger generation. The same concept can be applied everywhere from the boardroom to the PTA to Centre Court.

I have always known that someone else would eventually take my place in sports. I was thirteen when my parents taught me there will always be somebody better in the world than me. They always reminded me of that, no matter how good you are, it is not going to last forever, so enjoy your moment at the top (or whatever level) and make way for the youngsters when it's their turn. In sports we learn that very quickly, because our careers are relatively short and the risk of injury is always there, but it is true in every profession. You could be the best lawyer, CEO, executive assistant, nurse, architect, you name it—but eventually someone will come along and take your place or beat your record.

Studying history can help you achieve a healthy perspective when it comes to the passage of time. The more you know about history, the more you know about yourself, because it is the story of the human race. The generations are all connected as chapters of the same story. When I read about all these champions, I saw the inevitable changing of the guard. It is the rhythm of life. Of course, this is true for any profession, and once you accept and embrace the passing of the torch, it is much easier to be graceful and helpful to those coming after you. Each generation shapes the future for the next.

Arthur Ashe truly understood the importance of helping future generations. He not only impacted the lives of many by empowering young players—particularly players of color—giving them game advice, he was also proactive in connecting them with others who could help. When he contracted the AIDS virus, he became an activist on behalf of AIDS education and worked tirelessly to help slow the pandemic. Arthur also took a strong stand on human rights and particularly made a difference in the anti-apartheid struggle in South Africa. When we're motivated to make the world a better place, all our work is in some sense for those who come after us.

The idea of passing the torch and giving up your position on top can be a major source of anxiety for some people, but I look at it a different way. I *want* the young ones to do better than I did. Every generation sets the bar for the next, and every generation gets better. Because each generation encourages the next, the level of competition gets higher and higher.

Children watch you, but they think beyond you. For instance, young players kids who are watching Roger Federer or Serena Williams or Lindsay Davenport play tennis today are thinking, "I can be better than they are"—and they can be.

Passing the torch, symbolically or literally stepping out of the way, can be hard for some people, and it can be especially difficult to praise someone who is a competitor.

Each of us is leaving a legacy behind, whether we know it or not. And it can be a positive or negative one depending on the way we handle ourselves. The choice is ours: will we remain aware of the legacy we leave and be intentional about it? Or will we just focus on ourselves, on our own futures, and ignore how our lives impact those who come after us? It may be helpful to think about the kind of legacy you want to leave. Write a short legacy statement describing the way that you would like to be remembered, or the things you would like to be remembered for. Refer to it often and adjust it as necessary to regain perspective and focus in your life.

I remember when the media was touting Chris Evert as the new superstar player when she came into the game in the early 1970s, even though she was just a teenager. She also was the girl next door, which America loves. And if you were a veteran, as I was, it would have been easy to be jealous. She was young, popular, and a terrific athlete. She was my rival on the court and I wanted to defeat her—but I also did my best to support her off the court.

I knew Chris would take my place at the top of the women's game sooner or later—it was obvious by the way she played. Chris had something special: she loved pressure and rose to the occasion time after time. I wanted her to succeed. I remember telling people that she would be the next Number 1 player in the world—and she was the best in the world for seven years. People loved her, and that was great for tennis. Martina Navratilova, who later became the best singles, doubles, and mixed doubles player of all time, was right behind her. In fact, they were both terrific and had a fascinating, exciting rivalry that brought tennis a lot of positive exposure and a lot of new fans. (They both also became president of the Womens Tennis Association.)

The women players of my generation spent a lot of time mentoring Chris (and later, Martina), advising them on how to handle press conferences, how to act on the court, why it was important to attend sponsor parties and always keep their word. We taught them to promote other players as well as themselves. We always encouraged them, emphasizing that they were the next generation—the future of the sport we all loved. Their legacy was our legacy, their success was our success.

There is an added benefit in mentoring the next generation that many people may not see. Just as you can learn from your elders, you can also learn from younger people. There is a great line Rodgers and Hammerstein wrote in *The King and I*: "By your pupils you'll be taught." I know I learned from Chris and Martina, and so many others; they woke me up to new ideas, showed me how their generation is thinking. I learned as much as I taught them, if not more.

For instance, as young women of the next generation, Chris and Martina had higher expectations from the get-go about financial compensation and endorsements. They weren't satisfied with crumbs the women in my generation were receiving. They have set a new benchmark for the generations to come. Today's young women—in tennis and in general—aren't just hoping to be treated fairly and equally, they expect it. And this level of expectation is far higher, and more universally supported, than it was only a few decades ago. Progress has happened—the bar is set higher now. Their sense of entitlement and equality reinforces my own, and it is thrilling to see it come from them so naturally, when my generation had to cultivate it.

It is also important to make sure that the next generation is aware that they need to pass along their knowledge, too. We have a responsibility to teach each link in the chain how important it is to support the next link. While I mentored Chris and Martina, and later other girls, such as Tracy Austin, we kept reminding them that it was their job to mentor Steffi Graf and Monica Seles.

Although Chris and Martina were rivals for my spot at the top, the truth is that we had a great relationship when they were young and we still do to this day. I continue to mentor and befriend new generations of athletes and other rising stars, particularly through the Women's Sports Foundation, which mentors girls and women in more than 130 sports.

Each generation's job is to be on the cutting edge, to push the envelope for the next generation. A stronger connection between generations makes us all stronger. It makes us wiser and it improves our quality of life. I see leaving a legacy as building a wall; we left the wall one brick higher than the people before us, and the next generation is going to set another brick and make it even higher.

INSTANT REPLAY

Leave a Legacy

Part of leaving a worthy legacy is recognizing your role as just another link in the chain of life. Each of us has the ability to help lift up the next generation up, to be positive role models and to help young people pick up where we are leaving off. Passing the baton, encouraging young people to achieve more than we have, helps ensure that the quality of life can just keep improving for others long after we are gone.

Epilogue

Sheroes

and

Heroes

Everything came full circle in the late summer of 2006 during the U.S. Open at the USTA National Tennis Center in Flushing, New York, when I had the great honor of having that wonderful facility named after me. This would never have happened without the efforts of Franklin Johnson, the organization's president at the time, and the board of the USTA. I have been told it is the only major sports center in the world named after a woman. I wish there were more, but it feels great to me not because it is my name, but because of what it can mean to people to see a woman's name on one of the more important sports facilities in the country.

What I loved most about the ceremony that night was how my friends in tennis, including Chris Evert, Jimmy Connors, Venus Williams, and John McEnroe, came out and spoke about what the renaming meant to them. They all had wonderful messages to impart. One thing that particularly struck me was when McEnroe spoke about his transformation from not caring about Title IX and speaking out against equal-prize money for women to now having four daughters and caring very much about those issues. What a wonderful turn of events in his life, which mirrors the changing of minds throughout the country on these issues, especially from other Title IX dads. There is a whole generation of men now in their 40s and 50s who watched the Battle of the Sexes in 1973 and who, because of the influence of the Title IX effort in their younger years, insist that their sons and daughters be given equal opportunities in school and in life. We call these men the first generation of men in the women's movement. I have fathers approach me almost daily to tell me how the match changed their lives and changed how they raised, or are raising, their sons and daughters. This is one of the most gratifying offshoots of the Battle of the Sexes. My father was so important to me—he stood up for me and told me to go for my dreams. And because he allowed me to pursue my dreams, I was able to have this career and have the opportunity to fight for equality, which in turn has influenced other fathers to stand up for their daughters. Social change usually takes three generations to happen—how incredible that this change has happened in less than two!

I am proud of the fact that tennis has led the charge for social change over the years. Tennis always was a country-club sport in which we had to wear white and everyone was white. We even had to use white balls. But things started to change along racial lines with Althea Gibson and Arthur Ashe, two wonderful role models in our nation. Because men's and women's tennis was played in an organized way, side by side with the men almost from the start in tournaments, tennis had a head start in the women's movement over other women's sports. We also received more recognition: women's matches were always played during the same Grand Slam tournaments as men, so people got to know us as athletes.

It's wonderful to be looked up to, but it is also a great responsibility. Being a public figure, I have a chance to influence millions, but I think being a hero to one person is just as important as being a hero to many, and the same rules apply to both.

So many people who came before me have had such a lasting impact on my life. My parents and my brother, who were always supportive. My friends Susan Williams, who first introduced me to tennis, and Jerry Cromwell, with whom I played tennis almost every day (and to whom I once said, when we were kids, "you may be smarter than me, but I'm going to change the world through tennis"). Clyde Walker, who was my very first tennis instructor. I also was fortunate to have had four teachers—Mrs. Hunter and Mr. Bambrick at Los Cerritos Elementary School, Mr. Mays at Charles Evans Hughes Junior High School, and Mrs. Johnson from Long Beach Polytechnic High School—who taught me the importance of being supportive, having confidence, being a leader, and sharing my talents with others—because they shared theirs with me. Mervyn Rose had a huge impact on me—after I left college to get more serious about tennis, Bob Mitchell, an Australian businessman, brought me to Australia to work with Mervyn, who was a former Davis Cup player and was ranked in the top ten in the world five times in the 1950s. Taking lessons and playing with him totally changed my game and put the finishing touches on my style. Owen Davidson is another—a very dear

In 2007, I was there in the royal box at Wimbledon to watch Venus Williams accept the first-place trophy and a check for the same amount that the men's champion, Roger Federer, was paid the next day: about $1.4 million. It was the first time Wimbledon had offered equal prize money to both the men's and women's champion.

"No one loves tennis more than Billie Jean King," Venus said as the BBC interviewed her on Centre Court during the trophy presentation. She looked up at me in the box as the public address system carried her voice up to me. "I love you. I wouldn't be here if it weren't for you."

I waved to Venus, who was no more than 50 feet from me. She waved back. I could not help but smile on behalf of all my friends who signed that contract for $1 a decade before Venus was born. All those years of fighting for equal prize money, and when it finally happened at the most famous tennis club in the world, the woman who earned it truly understood why. And now she is one of the new leaders in the ongoing effort to achieve true equality in tennis and in other aspects of our culture.

friend and the only man with whom I ever won mixed doubles—four times, in fact, at Wimbledon. He really carried the load.

There have also been people who rose to hero status in my eyes because of their generosity and willingness to help me out, like Harold Guiver, who collected donations from the Long Beach Century Club, the Long Beach Tennis Patrons, and others to finance my trip to Wimbledon at age 17; or Dr. Joan Johnson, the womens tennis coach and Scotty Deeds, the mens tennis coach at Cal State LA. Because of those two coaches, the men and women practiced together three hours a day, almost every day.

The integrity, passion, compassion, generosity and kindness of these people are what I looked up to and what I have always tried to emulate. These are the things that determine who I consider my heroes. Each of my sheroes and heroes made me want to become a better person, which I think is the crux of being a hero in the first place. They were great role models for me.

I also was influenced by the Rev. Bob Richards, who was the pastor at my church, First Church of the Brethren, from the time I was 11 years old until I was 14. Rev. Richards had won a bronze medal in 1948 and two Olympic gold medals in 1952 and 1956 in the pole vault (in 1958, he was the first athlete to appear on the front of a Wheaties cereal box) and his wisdom and life advice were amazing. He managed to work sports metaphors into nearly every sermon, getting us all so worked up we believed we could do anything. He'd tell us sports stories with clear morals, instead of preaching to us about what we could or could not do. I also remember watching him work out in the field behind the church—he ran hurdles and practiced the pole vault almost every single day. I'd watch him and see the devotion he had to doing his best and just feel so inspired. I was thrilled to see him inducted into the Olympic Hall of Fame in 1983.

As a teenager I had the opportunity to work with the veteran player Alice Marble (who, incidentally, won the mixed doubles title with Bobby Riggs at Wimbledon in 1939). When I asked my coach, Clyde Walker, if I could go see her (it is proper protocol to get your coach's permission before seeking advice from other players or coaches, especially when you are young and still forming your game), he was ecstatic. He told me I would learn so much from her and I did. (Most coaches would never allow this today—they would feel threatened by it; but Clyde just wanted me to be happy.) Being around a Number 1 player taught me so many lessons—both on and off the court. For one thing, Alice was always very well-dressed and manicured. She said a champion should dress like a champion at all times. She spoke Spanish and could sing and play guitar, reminding me how important, not to mention enjoyable, it is to be a well-rounded person. She taught me to think more specifically about shots and strategy, and how important rituals are for maintaining focus during a game. Working with Alice, I became a stronger tennis player—I went from Number 19 in the country to Number 4 in 1960.

I live with the memories of these people to this day. Their influence on my life has shown me what kind of difference we can all make in the lives of others. Each generation stands on the shoulders of the pioneers who came before. I consider myself very lucky to have been blessed with the friendship of so many wonderful people. And if reading the lessons I have learned helps you improve your life and the lives of those around you in any way, then I am even more blessed.

Every person deserves the best life has to offer. Find out what inspires you, be good to yourself, keep dreaming your dreams, big and small, and go for it! But above all, I hope you enjoy the journey.

Acknowledgments

It takes a team to get things done, and we have been blessed to have a great group working in this project.

Without Ilana Kloss, my partner in life and in business, we would never have been able to complete this project.

Thanks to Tip Nunn, who lived this book with me.

My gratitude and appreciation go to the team at LifeTime Media who were my shepherds in this process and who kept me "in the book:" President Jacqueline Varoli Grace, Executive Editor Karyn Gerhard, and Publisher Kevin Moran. Thanks also to Roger Gorman and Judy McGuire of Reiner Design for all of their work to make this book look beautiful.

Christine Brennan brought her passion for women's sports and a commitment to make things better for future generations.

My dear friend Holly Hunter once again made me blush with her kind and beautiful words.

Acknowledgments

My special thanks to the Alter family, the Woolard family, Paula Polito, and Ann Moore for believing in me and my dream.

Thanks to Russ Adams, the godfather of all tennis photographers, and to Susan and Fred Mullane, for the beautiful images in this book.

Thanks to Rosie Casals, a great friend who took the heat in the broadcasting booth at the match and was a giant doubles partner through the years.

To Larry King, who was so instrumental behind the scenes of the Battle of the Sexes and who understood the real significance of the match.

My thanks to Lornie Kuhle, who has continued Bobby Riggs's legacy, for providing us with important background on the match and, more importantly, for being my dear friend.

To "Team Billie Jean"—Diane Stone, Barbara Perry, Merle Blackman, and Rich Blackman—thanks for keeping my business life moving forward.

Thanks to my associates at World TeamTennis—Rosie Crews, Jeff Harrison, Jennel Hewan, Bryan Hicks, Delaine Mast, Rory Paolantonio, Jessie Rybacki, Kerry Schneider, Samantha Shaw, Jen Smith, Jason Spitz and Elaine Wingfield—who kept our real business running smoothly.

Finally, to the countless people in my life who have made a difference in our world, I thank you for your inspiration, your willingness to help others, and your commitment to doing the right thing.

In my last conversation with Bobby Riggs, before he passed away, he said to me, "Billie, we really made a difference, didn't we." Looking back, he was right. It was a privilege to have shared that moment in history with him.

Captions

Page 6: Preparing to serve during the Battle of the Sexes.

Page 18: With Bobby Riggs at the press conference announcing the Battle of the Sexes.

Page 34: Left to right: Susan Williams, Jerry Cromwell, Alan Robbins, and me, circa 1955.

Page 46: As a child outside our home in Long Beach, California, circa 1949.

Page 60: Hitting a forehand during the match.

Page 76: Surveying the surroundings at the Astrodome the afternoon before the match.

Page 90: Bobby Riggs and his "bosom buddies."

Page 98: Celebrating my victory.

Page 114: The scoreboard during the final game of the match.

Page 120: Bobby congratulating me.

Page 128: Arriving in the Astrodome aboard the Egyptian litter.

Page 142: With members of the Original Nine, holding up our $1 contractual payment.

Page 158: At the U.S. Open ceremony to rename The USTA National Tennis Center the USTA Billie Jean King National Tennis Center, August 28, 2006.

Page 166: Signing autographs for young tennis fans at a World TeamTennis match, 2007.

Page 178: With my partner, Ilana Kloss, and my mother, Betty Moffitt, at the U.S. Open renaming ceremony.

Photo Credits

Pages 6, 18, 60, 76, 90, 98, 114, 120, 124: Photos © Russ Adams
Pages 34, 46: Photos courtesy Billie Jean King
Pages 158, 166, 178: Photo by Susan Mullane/Camerawork USA
Page 142: Photo courtesy the Sony Ericsson WTA Tour